CULTURES OF THE WORLD

Niger

Rabah Seffal and Jo-Ann Spilling

mc **Marshall Cavendish**
Benchmark
New York

PICTURE CREDITS
Cover: © Bruno Morandi/Getty Images
Alamy/Bes Stock: 18 • Alamy/Photolibrary: 8, 12, 17, 37, 38, 39, 42, 43, 48, 49, 51, 55, 56, 57, 59, 60 ,61, 62,
68, 72, 76, 79, 81, 85, 86, 87, 88, 89, 90, 92, 95, 100, 102, 103, 105, 112, 114, 115, 117, 121, 122, 124, 128, 129
• alt.type/Reuters: 30, 31, 33, 52, 53, 98, 119 • Associated Press: 25 • Audrius Tomonis: 135 • Corbis: 24, 34,
47, 69, 84, 116 • David Beatty/AFP/Getty Images: 106 • Francis Tan: 130, 131 • Getty Images: 26, 27, 29, 32,
35, 36, 45, 65, 66, 77, 78, 80, 91, 96, 97, 109, 113, 120, 125, 127 • Hutchison Library: 9, 19, 40, 41, 64, 70, 71,
74, 75, 83, 94 • Lonely Planet Images: 82, 93, 104, 111, 123 • Nik Wheeler: 108, 126 • Photolibrary: 1, 3, 5, 6,
10, 11, 13, 14, 15, 16, 22, 44, 46, 50, 54, 58, 63, 67, 73, 101, 110 • Topfoto: 23

PRECEDING PAGE
A traditional village in Bouza, Niger.

Publisher (U.S.): Michelle Bisson
Editors: Deborah Grahame, Mindy Pang
Copyreader: Tara Tomczyk
Designers: Nancy Sabato, Benson Tan
Cover picture researcher: Connie Gardner
Picture researcher: Thomas Khoo

Marshall Cavendish Benchmark
99 White Plains Road
Tarrytown, NY 10591
Website: www.marshallcavendish.us

© Times Media Private Limited 2000
© Marshall Cavendish International (Asia) Private Limited 2011
® "Cultures of the World" is a registered trademark of Times Publishing Limited.

Originated and designed by Times Media Private Limited
An imprint of Marshall Cavendish International (Asia) Private Limited
A member of Times Publishing Limited

Marshall Cavendish is a trademark of Times Publishing Limited.

All Internet sites were correct and accurate at the time of printing. All monetary figures in this publication
are in U.S. dollars.

Library of Congress Cataloging-in-Publication Data
Seffal, Rabah.
  Niger / Rabah Seffal and Jo-Ann Spilling. — 2nd ed.
    p. cm. — (Cultures of the world)
  Includes bibliographical references and index.
  Summary: "Provides comprehensive information on the geography, history,
    wildlife, governmental structure, economy, cultural diversity, peoples,
    religion, and culture of Niger"—Provided by publisher.
  ISBN 978-1-60870-026-4
  1. Niger—Juvenile literature. I. Spilling, Jo-Ann. II. Title.
  DT547.22.S44 2010
  966.26—dc22   2010001209

Printed in China
7 6 5 4 3 2 1

CONTENTS

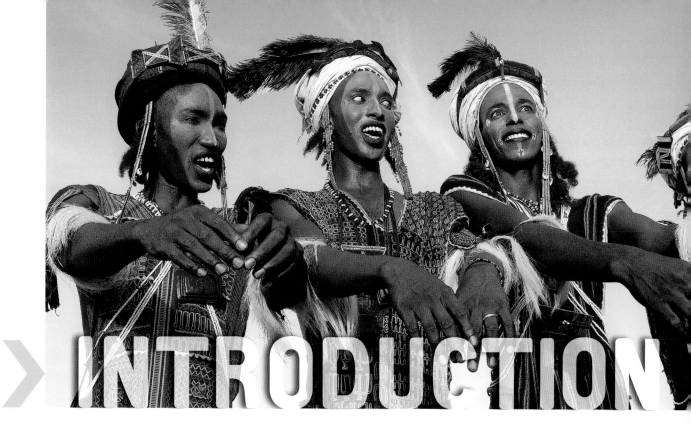

INTRODUCTION

THE REPUBLIC OF NIGER IS A LANDLOCKED country situated in Western Africa. It is one of the largest but poorest countries in Africa, with a rapidly growing population of approximately 15 million. Taking its name from the Niger River, the country shares borders with several African neighbors—Nigeria and Benin to the south, Burkina Faso and Mali to the west, Algeria and Libya to the north, and Chad to the east. Niger is also one of the hottest places on Earth. Over 80 percent of the country is occupied by the Sahara desert. Temperatures can sometimes reach 113°F (45°C). The economy is mainly based on agriculture, although the country has enjoyed gains from the export of uranium and, more recently, oil. In spite of its natural resources, Niger remains undeveloped due to its landlocked position, recurring drought, weak infrastructure, and the poor level of education and health among its people. In 1960 Niger gained independence from French colonial rule. Nigerien society is diverse and consists of six major ethnic groups—the Hausa, the Songhai, and Djerma, the Peuhl, the Tuareg, and the Kanouri (Kanuri). The majority is made up of Muslims and most people live in rural communities. Those who live in urban areas are clustered in the south of the country, in the capital city of Niamey, and other cities such as Maradi, Agadez, and Zinder.

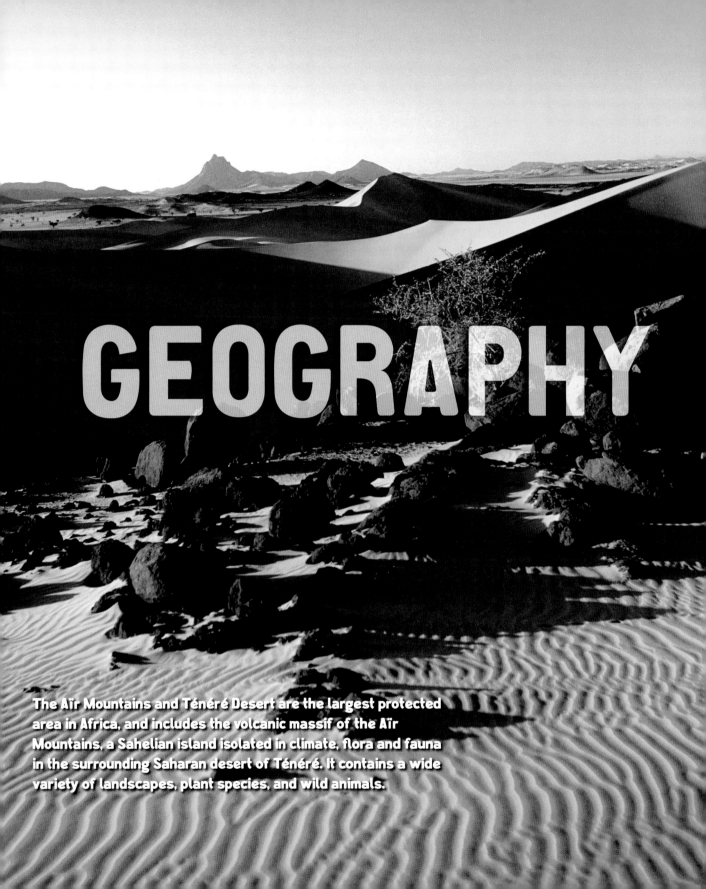

GEOGRAPHY

The Aïr Mountains and Ténéré Desert are the largest protected area in Africa, and includes the volcanic massif of the Aïr Mountains, a Sahelian island isolated in climate, flora and fauna in the surrounding Saharan desert of Ténéré. It contains a wide variety of landscapes, plant species, and wild animals.

CHAPTER 1

THE REPUBLIC OF NIGER IS THE second-largest country in West Africa and Africa's sixth-largest country. Its total land area is twice the size of Texas. Along with Mali and Burkina Faso, Niger is one of three landlocked countries on the African continent.

Niger's neighbors include Algeria to the northwest, Libya to the northeast, Chad to the east, Nigeria to the south, Benin and Burkina Faso to the southwest, and Mali to the west. Because the north and northeast are arid and thus largely uninhabitable, Niger's population is concentrated in the southern part of the country.

TOPOGRAPHY

Niger is located north of Africa's belt of tropical forest. Most of the country is desert. Although it is primarily a flat plain, the country has several depressions, plateaus, sandy lowlands, fossilized river valleys, and volcanic mountains.

Niger is naturally divided into three distinct regions: the south, the Sahelian belt, and the desert north. The southwest region near the Niger River has an average altitude of 1,067 feet (325 meters) above sea level. The arid transitional center, called the Sahel, has seasonal rainfall and is most suitable for nomadic animal husbandry. It separates the fertile land of the Niger River Valley from the harsh desert of the north. The north includes the Aïr Mountains and the plateaus of Djado, Tchigaï, and Mangueni, as well as the Saharan sandy lowlands surrounding the Aïr Mountains.

Niger has a total
land area of
488,946 square
miles (1,266,700
square kilometers).

THE SOUTH

The south, which includes the fertile region around the Niger River, consists of a broad plain with an area of 46,320 square miles (119,969 square km), or about 10 percent of the total land area of Niger. The altitude in this area varies between 985 and 1,149 feet (between 300 and 350 m) above sea level. Because this is the country's most intensively cultivated area, the population density in the south averages about 200 people per square miles (76 per square km). The overall average density for the entire country is only 29 people per square miles (11 per square km), as the north of Niger is sparsely populated.

To the southeast Niger's territory includes 988 square miles (2,559 square km) of Lake Chad, Africa's fourth-largest lake, which Niger shares with Nigeria and Chad. Lying along part of the border with Nigeria is the Komadugu-Yobe River, which flows into Lake Chad.

A man rowing a small boat across Lake Chad in Niger at sunset.

A camel train
crossing the desert
in the Sahel.

THE SAHEL

Separating the desertlike north from the fertile south is the Sahel, an arid region with very little rainfall. *Sahel* means "shore" in Arabic—the area is the shore of the "sea of sand" of the Sahara. This region is usually divided into the north Sahel belt, which includes the city of Agadez, and the south Sahel belt. Agricultural activities in the Agadez region are only possible in oases. The south Sahel belt has a rainfall pattern that allows crops to be grown for four months of the year. The area also supports grazing for the cattle of nomadic herders. Although the Sahel belts can be relatively self-sufficient in good rainfall years, during severe droughts its inhabitants suffer greatly.

THE NORTH

In the north of the Sahel and the city of Agadez lie the spectacular Aïr Mountains, a southern extension of the Algerian Ahaggar Mountains. The

A gazelle in a sandstorm in the Sahara.

Aïr Mountains contain many rock paintings made by Stone Age people. With an area of approximately 30,880 square miles (79,979 square km) and an average elevation of up to 2,625 feet (800 m), the Aïr Mountains are intersected by several ravines where date palms, dum-dum palms, and desert bushes flourish. In the Aïr, Mount Gréboun is Niger's highest peak. It towers at 6,380 feet (1,945 m).

East of the Aïr Mountains is the Ténéré, which means "desert" in Tamasheqt, the language of the Tuareg people. The total area of the Ténéré is 154,400 square miles (399,896 square km). It offers a magnificent landscape of sand dunes that seem to stretch to the horizon. Tuareg caravans from Agadez still travel to the oases that punctuate the Ténéré dunes, trading for salt.

To the west of the Aïr, the Talak Desert consists of shifting sand dunes interrupted by ancient river valleys, similar to those found in the Aïr Mountains. About 6,000 years ago water used to flow in these valleys, allowing the desert north of Niger to support a larger population. Now the grasslands of this region attract nomadic cattle herders, but only during the short rainy seasons.

Northeast of the Ténéré lie the high plateaus of Djado and Tchigaï, and the Mangueni Mountains, an extension of the Tibesti Mountains of Chad to the east and the Ahaggar Mountains of Algeria to the north. These highlands form a bridge linking the two mountain systems.

CLIMATE AND RAINFALL

Niger is one of the hottest countries in the world. It has three climatic regions: the desert north, the Sahel, and the south. The desert north, including the Ténéré, receives little rainfall, thus offering neither agricultural nor cattle herding possibilities except in oases and the old river valleys of the Talak. South of the desert, the north Sahel has a maximum of 14 inches

The highly variable climate of the Sahel poses a threat to the long-term survival of its inhabitants. During the 19th century the human and animal populations grew rapidly due to a higher-than-normal rainfall. Then the Sahel suffered a severe drought between 1911 and 1915, which killed more than 350,000 people in central Niger alone.

Even after the country gained independence in 1960, the situation did not improve. From 1968 to 1973 another drought wiped out livestock and crippled the social and economic system of the area, especially that of the nomadic herders. The drought effects included food shortages in following years. Again in 1984 and 2004, severe droughts brought extensive suffering to the country.

(36 centimeters) of annual rainfall. In Agadez annual rainfall does not exceed 7 inches (18 cm). The south Sahel receives 12 to 32 inches (30—81 cm) of rainfall per year. In the south, a rainy season from June to October is preceded by violent tornadoes. In the extreme south, around Gaya, rainfall averages 32 inches (81 cm) per year.

During the dry season, from January to October, temperatures are very high. From November the temperature starts to drop, falling as low as 46°F (26°C) in January. In November a desert wind, called the harmattan, lowers average temperatures to 70°F (39°C). Reddish sandstorms sweep across the country during this period. From February to July the dry and hot season sets in, with temperatures reaching a scorching 122°F (68°C) in the northeast.

FLORA AND FAUNA

Because of Niger's climate, flora and fauna vary dramatically from the dry north to the wetter and more fertile south. Similar to its Sahelian neighbors, Niger is suffering from ecological degradation. Irregular rainfall and periodic droughts threaten animal populations and plant life of Niger.

Shrubs growing in the Erg du Bilma desert in Niger.

The desert north, which covers 60 percent of Niger's land surface, has little vegetation. However, in Bilma, abundant springs allow some tree species, such as eucalypti, to flourish. On the northern rim of the Aïr Mountains, several types of Mediterranean plants, such as Laperrine olive and cypresses, have survived. In the Sahel thorns, *Mimoseae, Graminaceae*, and scattered pastures of grass have a short life and provide good grazing material for both nomadic and settled herds. A useful plant is the *areleshem*, sought after by camels. The areleshem has oval-shaped leaves and white, budlike flowers. The Tuareg use the *areleshem* flowers as a cure for stomachaches. To the south, denser vegetation is found, including baobab trees, silk cotton, mahogany, and shea trees.

In the north the lack of water and vegetation, coupled with extremely high temperatures, limits the types of wildlife. The largest animal found is the one-humped camel. Its broad, leathery footpads are well adapted to the desert. Besides the domesticated camel, wild animals, such as antelopes and gazelles, are found in the Ténéré and the Aïr regions. These animals are the favorite prey of leopards, striped hyenas, and jackals.

The smaller desert animals in Niger include desert foxes or fennecs, which prey on jerboas or desert mice. The sensitive fennec has large, pointed ears and can hear a desert beetle kick over grains of sand several yards away. Moufflons can be found in the inaccessible terrain of the Aïr Mountains and Djado Plateau. South of the Sahara, ostriches, the world's tallest birds, live in hot, sandy areas. The males are polygamous and travel in multifamily groups. Eggs are laid in sandy depressions and incubated by females during the day, and by males at night. Desert animals eat a large number of insects, including the migratory locusts, as well as scorpions and vipers.

A desert or fennec fox adult resting on a warm desert afternoon.

Although droughts and poaching have taken their toll on Niger's wildlife, some large mammals, such as elephants, giraffes, and hippopotami, and reptiles and amphibians still exist. The nature reserve and wildlife refuge of the "W" National Park is home to monkeys, baboons, hyenas, jackals, lions, elephants, buffalos, antelopes, and gazelles. Birdlife, including the brown crow, is also abundant there. The nomads herd cattle, sheep, goats, donkeys, and camels. Camels are also used as a means of transportation by caravans, especially by the salt traders.

MAJOR CITIES

NIAMEY The city derives its name from the term *Way niammané*, which means "settle and acquire." *Way niammané* was an order given by a Djerma leader named Kallé to his subjects when they saw a vast uninhabited region next to the river. The city was first named Niamma and then Niamey. In 1926 a French general saw the strategic potential of Niamey as the capital. Access to the river and the moderate climate in this city made the French transfer their administrative capital from Zinder to Niamey. Until then Niamey was not an economically or politically important city.

Cars parked at Niamey city. Niger's capital, Niamey, is located along the fertile strip of land bordering the 300-mile-long (483-km-long) Niger River.

Niamey began as a grouping of several villages that grew and joined to become one city. In 1905 the population was only 1,800. It grew to 7,000 in 1945. Today, with a population of 900,000, Niamey is a sprawling modern center with shantytowns on the outskirts. Beautiful villas can be found in the residential areas next to the ministerial offices. Traditional-style African houses also neatly line the streets.

ZINDER With a population of 200,000 people, Zinder is a typical Hausa town with a narrow maze of alleys. Connected to Niamey by a monotonous 450-mile (724-km) "unity road," it is generally regarded as the second-most important city in Niger. Several roads connect Zinder with the city of Kano in Nigeria. A few small industries are located in Zinder. They concentrate on the processing of farm products and the manufacturing of small industrial products.

The neighborhood of Zengou, in Zinder, is a former caravan encampment. Until the 1890s Zinder was Niger's only major urban settlement, with a population of about 10,000. Built around a citadel, it was a major point of exchange and storage for the trans-Saharan trade route. Precolonial Zinder was home to the Hausa kingdom of Damagram, which was a strong economic power. In 1898 the French captain, Cazemajou, on a mission to neutralize Zinder, was killed. Zinder put up a heavy resistance to French invasion, ultimately falling in 1899. It remained the administrative capital of the French military territory of Niger until 1926. An old French Foreign Legion fort still stands in the city today.

AGADEZ Located in the Aïr Mountains, about 400 miles (644 km) northeast of Niamey, Agadez was the ancient Tuareg capital. The city still preserves its trading caravans and the myths surrounding that life. It is a town built at the edge of the desert that serves as the link between the free but treacherous desert life and the limited but safe urban life. The Hausa of Gobir, who fled Tuareg raiders in the sixth century, live in Agadez. The trans-Saharan gold trade route to North Africa passed through Agadez and brought prosperity and strength to local rulers. The Empire of Mali occupied Agadez for 50 years from 1325. The city fell to the powerful Songhai Empire in the 1515. Sultans El-Mobarak and Agaba ruled Agadez from 1654 to 1721. In 1906 the French occupied the city.

Today Agadez is a meeting point for all Tuareg groups and a living center for the preservation of their ancient history. With a population of 88,569, Agadez is sometimes referred to as the sister city of Timbuktu in Mali. The color of its distinctive sand-brick architecture matches that of the desert dunes. Its people are mainly Tuareg, but the population also includes Fulani nomads and Hausa merchants.

An aerial view of Agadez. The population of Agadez increased significantly after the discovery of uranium, which boosted the economy of the north.

HISTORY

The ancient mosque of Agadez,
built of mud in the 16th century.

NIGER HAS HAD A LONG, tumultuous history. From ethnic struggles to independence, the country has faced many years of foreign dominance and civil strife.

EARLY INHABITANTS

Stone tools, evidence of a Paleolithic culture, indicate the presence of humans more than 60,000 years ago in the Aïr, Ténéré, Djado, and Kuwar regions. The stone tools, including axes, oval disks used for cutting and scraping, and stone knives, were produced by a Neolithic Saharan culture that domesticated bulls and herded cattle—an activity that is still practiced today by the different nomadic groups of Niger. Artists of the Neolithic Saharan culture probably drew the numerous rock paintings that are often found north of Agadez.

Prehistoric rock paintings found near the Oasis of Tezizet in the Aïr Mountains. Many of these rock paintings depicted cattle, hunters using chariots, and horsemen.

THE SAVANNAH KINGDOMS

THE ZAGHAWA KINGDOM was located around the Chad Basin from A.D. 700 to 1100 and occupied the North Kanem region, northeast of Lake Chad. The term *Zaghawa* does not refer to a specific culture or period but to the pre-Islamic black inhabitants of the region. The Zaghawa were the first to acquire the skill to cast iron, make crafts, and provide services to the nomadic and sedentary groups around Kanem. They relied on agriculture, fishing, and making crafts for a living, and in a later period, they engaged in international trade, which included slaves, with the Muslim states of North Africa and the Middle East. An economic transformation led to the rise of the Kanem Empire after the 12th century.

THE HABASHA KINGDOM was predominantly made out of Chadic speakers, who lived on the river valleys around the same time as the Zaghawa. Similar to the Zaghawa, the Habasha traded and sold their agricultural produce as well as other crafts and were not just subsistence farmers. Most were cattle herders and salt traders. The Habasha did not have territorial aspirations.

An artist's impression of early Niger.

Southern Niger was part of west Sudan when gold was traded between the Muslim and Sudanese traders. Although the Muslim traders were involved in the gold trade, their Sudanese counterparts supplied them with little information about the location of the gold mines. Muslim geographers used to say that gold grew in the sand of Sudan as carrots did. The Sudanese had an equally unusual trading relationship with their gold suppliers from the gold-producing center in the south of Niger. Known as the silent auction, this method of barter illustrated their peculiar trading customs. The Sudanese traders would place their merchandise, mainly salt bars from the Sahara, in piles on the bank of the river and then retreat. Afterward the local people would appear with their gold and would place some gold next to each pile of merchandise and then withdraw. The traders would return to the riverbank and take the gold if the amount placed against each pile satisfied them. They would then disappear. The local people would emerge from their hiding places and go to the riverbank to collect the merchandise they had bought.

As the Zaghawa kingdom expanded to the west, the Habasha kingdom contracted into the kingdoms of Gobir and Katsina. As the Mbau tribe on the southern border developed, the Habasha joined them to form what was later known as the Mbau kingdom. The term *Mbau* refers to the original inhabitants of the savannah region between Niger and Nigeria. Although traces of their history are found today in the numerous village names, their language is now almost extinct. The Mbau people were much feared for their raids.

Many of the settlements of the early kingdoms were located along the Niger River.

Toward the seventh-century A.D., the first Songhai and Kanem states appeared in the western and the eastern parts of Niger, respectively. From the core of Mali, the Songhai Empire expanded its territory along the Niger

THE SONGHAI EMPIRE *was one of the greatest empires of West Africa. Its dominance reached a peak when Sonni Ali took power and lasted more than 100 years. The dominant individuals of the Songhai were the Sorko fishermen. Known as the masters of waters, the Sorko navigated the waters of Niger River from Dendi, reaching places north of Tillabéry. A cohesive and important political organization was born among them, resulting in the first Songhai dynasty known as the Dya. By the eighth century* A.D., *increased economic relations with the Kharedjite Tahert state in western Algeria strengthened the Songhai kingdom. The city of Gao became the commercial center and the residence of the Songhai rulers. Kukiya, southeast of Gao, remained the ancestral capital, where festivals and royal celebrations took place.*

Around the mid-12th century the Empire of Mali attempted to extend its rule over all Saharan trade route terminals. However, as a remote province, Songhai attempted to gain its independence amid periods of weakness in Mali. Under the leadership of Ali Kolon, the new dynasty of the Sonni was founded. But it was not until the beginning of the 15th century that the Songhai Empire started to build its military power and begin expansion under the rule of Sonni Ali the Great (1464—92). Spreading westward, it conquered Timbuktu in 1469 and Jene in 1473. As the Empire of Mali retreated south of the Niger Delta, having lost its Sahelian territory, the Songhai Empire, during the rule of Askia Muhammad (1493—1528), took over additional provinces that had been part of Mali. It also conquered the Berber city of Agadez and the Hausa states on the southern border of today's Niger. The end of the 15th century saw the destruction of the Songhai Empire when the North African empire of Morocco conquered its territory.

River, while the Kanem Empire concentrated its rule around Lake Chad and extended its conquest north to the Fezzan in Libya. In between the two empires, smaller states, such as the Hausa states, emerged. Around A.D. 1000, an increase in economic relations with North Africa via the Aïr region led to migrations of Tuareg from Libya and Algeria toward the Aïr and adjacent regions. At this time, both the Songhai and Kanem empires adopted Islam as their religion. Meanwhile, the Hausa, who previously lived in the north, gradually moved south.

THE EMPIRE OF BORNU benefited greatly from the collapse of the Kanem Empire. The latter empire fell due to the lack of resources, royal rivalry, and internal conflicts, which erupted in the mid-13th century. Even before the collapse of Kanem, parts of Bornu had become independent, especially after the Bornu economy started to benefit from the direct trans-Saharan trade route to North Africa. In the 14th century, when the Suffewa rulers started to encounter opposition from the Bulala, a rival dynasty, the Suffewa rulers and their followers left Kanem and headed toward Bornu, where they had long before placed lords.

Even though the Suffewa fled from Kanem, their conflict with the Bulala continued for many years. The Suffewa later solved their internal problems and regained strength and security from 1465 to 1497 under the rule of Ali Dunama, also called Ghaji "the Younger." He was able to resolve the struggle for the throne between the different branches of the Suffewa. In addition, Ali Ghaji ended the threat of the Bulala once and for all and laid the foundation of a new and powerful Suffewa Mais dynasty, with its capital at Ngazargamu. The Suffewa in Bornu saw in Islam a powerful means of strengthening their authority over the Bornu lands. As the different groups accepted Islam, stability was restored.

THE 16TH TO 19TH CENTURIES

In the 16th century the region that was to become Niger was greatly influenced by the Songhai and Bornu empires. The Bornu Empire reached its apex under the rule of Idris Alauma (1564—76). The acme of Songhai rule occurred during the reign of Askia Mohammed (1493—1528). In 1498 Askia Mohammed went on a pilgrimage to the Muslim holy city of Mecca. On completing his pilgrimage to Mecca, he received the two honored titles— al Hajj and the Caliph of the Western Sudan—which increased his support among the Songhai Muslims and helped consolidate his rule.

The Songhai Empire was destroyed by Moroccans who came to search for the gold of Sudanic Africa, and who wanted to control the trade routes. The Battle of Tondibi in 1591 was a heavy loss for the Songhai; it was their

Zinder was the capital of the Damagaran state. In the mid-19th century, its ruler, Ténimoum, erected a 3-mile (5-km) wall around the city. According to legend, this majestic wall would never collapse because a number of Korans, the Muslim holy book, and virgin girls were "built" into the walls. Over the years, the wall has broken down, and all that remains are ruins.

first encounter with the use of gunpowder and muskets. Nine years later the Moroccans were forced out of Dendi. Despite this the Songhai Askia dynasty soon collapsed and fragmented into smaller and weaker states. The Songhai Empire never regained its previous grandeur.

In the 19th century the Hausa state of Damagaran in the east became a great military and economic power. Zinder was their capital, and manufacturing and new agricultural products were introduced during this period of time.

THE TUAREG DOMINATION

As a result of an improved economy spurred by the trade routes through the Sahara, the influence of the Tuareg grew. They established their first sultanate in the Aïr Mountains as early as the beginning of 15th century. Agadez, in the southern part of the Aïr Mountains, became an economic and cultural center, attracting merchants from North Africa. As the center grew in economic importance, the role of the Tuareg became more of an arbiter than a guardian of the caravan traffic. Their control stretched to Gao and Timbuktu in the west and to Tadmakka in Mali.

Tuareg at the Valley of Aouderas in 18th-century Niger.

In the Aïr Mountains, from 1654 to 1687, the Tuaregs were ruled by Muhammad Al-Mubarak, who extended his authority to the Damergou region. He also established a branch of the Agadez dynasty that became the empire of Sarkin Adar in the late 17th century. As Tuareg dominance grew, there were frequent internal conflicts, which divided them into several factions. But as they gained control of more regions, they started to appreciate the advantages of being a large-scale organization.

A painting of veiled Tuareg nomads in the Sahara.

THE FRENCH CONQUEST

In the 19th century, as a prelude to their conquest, Europeans started to explore Niger. In 1890 an agreement between France and Great Britain at a meeting with King Leopold II of Belgium established the border between what was to become Niger and Nigeria. The partitioning of Africa was an attempt to set out spheres of influence and avoid the threat of war among European countries that were eager to gain control over Africa's resources such as gold and diamonds. France then started its conquest of the country but met with strong resistance. In 1898 Sultan Ahmadu Kuren Daga ordered the execution of French captain Cazemajou.

Subsequent armed exploration by French captains Paul Voulet and Charles Chanoine resulted in bloody massacres and the destruction of cities and villages, before the country was conquered. Throughout the years of French domination, the local population continued to fight the French. The Zarama uprising (1905—6) and the Tuareg resistance (1916—17) resulted in much bloodshed. British troops were brought in to assist the French, and the Tuareg suffered a major defeat. In 1922, when peace was finally restored, Niger became a French colony.

ROAD TO INDEPENDENCE

Niger was administered from Paris through the governor-general in Dakar, Senegal. The lack of natural resources in Niger limited French investment, compared with other French West African colonies. As France decentralized its political power after World War II, Nigeriens were theoretically granted full citizenship in 1946. However, their participation in local politics was limited.

A nationalist movement soon gained momentum. In a split in the early 1950s, two groups formed—a radical group with a strong trade union, led by Djibo Bakary, and a more conservative movement, the Nigerien Progressive Party, that supported Hamani Diori. Diori won the Territorial Assembly elections in 1957. He formed a government and banned Bakary's Sawaba Party. On September 28, 1958, the Nigerien population approved the constitution of General Charles De Gaulle's Fifth French Republic. On December 19, 1958, Niger's Territorial Assembly voted for Niger to become an autonomous state within the French community, to be called the Republic of Niger. On August 3, 1960, Niger declared its independence.

African leaders (*from left to right*) Hubert Maga of Dahomey, Yameogo of Upper Volta, Felix Houphouet Boigny of Ivory Coast, and Hamani Diori of Niger). pose at the door of the Elysee Palace after seeing President De Gaulle of France about their full independence in 1960.

AFTER INDEPENDENCE

When Niger gained its independence, Hamani Diori was elected Niger's first president by the country's national assembly in November 1960. The first Nigerien constitution was approved on November 8, 1960. As the sole party, the Niger Progressive Party (PPN) became firmly established throughout the country, including the rural areas. The government's program of political democratization was resisted by students and civil service groups. The drought of 1973 dealt a severe blow to the economy, and internal problems remained unsolved. On April 15, 1974, Lieutenant Colonel Seyni Kountché staged a military coup. He succeeded in suspending the constitution, dissolving the PPN, and arresting its leaders. Diori was replaced by Kountché.

Lieutenant Colonel
Seyni Kountché.

Kountché formed a provisional government, which was led by the Supreme Military Council. He maintained cordial relations with France, Niger's former colonizer, despite the fact that he expelled French troops. The late 1980s saw a significant increase in revenue from uranium, which allowed Niger to recover financially from the drought. Following Kountché's death in 1987, Colonel Ali Seybou was appointed president after the adoption of a new constitution that returned civilians to power, although Niger remained a one-party state.

In November 1991 the transitional government of Amadou Acheffou replaced President Seybou. The Tuaregs revolted in the north amid rumors that the government had embezzled international funds meant for the resettlement of the Tuareg population who had fled during the severe droughts. Both parties consequently signed several peace treaties, but the truces were short-lived. In January 1996 Colonel Ibrahim Baré Maïnassara overthrew the elected government of Mahamane Ousmane, putting an end to democracy. He was elected president in July with 52 percent of the vote. Maïnassara was assassinated on April 9, 1999, at the Niamey airport. A National Reconciliation Council was formed, and Commandant Daouda Malam Wanké became the president of Niger on April 11, 1999. A few months later in October 1999, Mamadou Tandja from the MNSD (National Movement for the Development of Society) party was elected president but was ousted by the military during the February 2010 coup d'état.

GOVERNMENT

ASSEMBLEE NATIONALE

The Nigerien National Assembly building.

CHAPTER 3

AFTER NIGER GAINED its independence in 1960, the country was run by the PPN (*Parti Progressiste Nigérien*), under the leadership of Hamani Diori. He consolidated party power by banning the opposition party, the Sawaba.

The 1970 drought, coupled with protests started by unions and students, weakened the government, which was overthrown by a military coup in 1974. In 1989 presidential and legislative elections were held for the newly formed National Movement for the Development of Society (MNSD) to anchor its power.

A man holds a banner reading "Long life to Niger's army. Long life to CSRD. Yes to the restoration of democracy" during a rally in support of their new military rulers after the 2010 coup ousted President Mamadou Tandja.

Since its independence in 1960, the Republic of Niger has had five constitutions, two major constitutional revisions, and two periods of rule by decree. Niger operates a multiparty system, with two to three strong parties and smaller parties elected to assume seats in the National Assembly. These smaller parties usually enter into electoral coalitions with their more powerful opponents.

However, Tuareg revolts and attacks, student demonstrations, and union and civil society unrest forced the government to hold a free, multiparty election in 1993. In 1996 the Nigerien armed forces staged a coup, claiming they were saving the country from disintegration, the result of a paralyzed political system. In July 1996, Ibrahim Baré Maïnassara became the new president of Niger. He was assassinated by his bodyguards in 1999, and Major Daouda Wanké assumed power. In late 1999 the MNSD won the majority of seats in parliament, and Mamadou Tandja was elected president. He won a second term in office in 2004. In August 2009, amid protests, Mamadou Tandja won a referendum that would allow him to rule for another three years.

LOCAL GOVERNMENT

The country is divided into seven territorial units called *departments* (day-PART-mahn) and one capital district, Niamey. The departments are subdivided into 38 districts, called *arrondissements* (ah-RAWN-dees-mahn), and are run by a chief administrator, called a *prefet* (PRAY-fay). The *prefet* is appointed by the central government in Niamey and acts as the departments' local agent.

THE PRESIDENT

The current constitution, approved in a referendum, provides for the election of a president with executive powers for a five-year term. He can stay in office for a maximum of two terms. Elected by popular vote, the president is both the chief of state and head of the government. He appoints a prime minister and a 26-member cabinet of ministers on the recommendation of the prime minister.

The right of the Nigeriens to elect their government was granted in the 1993 constitution. Nevertheless the January 1996 military coup, subsequent presidential elections, and a constitutional referendum election prevented Nigeriens from fully exercising that right. One of the most important constitutional changes in 1993 was an increase in the power of the president.

The president rules by decree when the National Assembly is not in session. The executive branch appoints members of the judiciary, officials of the security forces, and heads of state-owned companies. The legislative branch is the unicameral National Assembly, which has 113 members who are elected for five-year terms. The president can initiate legislation either by proposing an act to the National Assembly or by submitting it to a popular referendum.

THE CONSTITUTION

On November 8, 1960, the constitution of an independent Niger was officially published establishing a presidential regime. Following the coup in 1974, this constitution was suspended, and the National Assembly was dissolved. All executive and legislative power was held by the Supreme Military Council until 1989. In 1993 a new constitution was adopted. When the government was overthrown by Colonel Ibrahim Maïnassara in 1996, the constitution was revised by national referendum on May 12, 1996. Today Niger operates under the constitution of July 18, 1999. The current constitution restores the semi-presidential system of government of the 1992 constitution in which the president of the republic is elected by universal suffrage for a five-year term, and a prime minister, chosen by the president, shares executive power.

The seven departments include Agadez, Diffa, Dosso, Maradi, Tahoua, Tillaberi, and Zinder.

A traditional Nigerien chief at a conference.

The Nigerien constitution separates church and state, and guarantees the political, cultural, and religious freedom of its citizens, with the right to form associations. Under the constitution all languages have equal status as national languages, although French is the official language. Nigeriens have the freedom to travel in and out of the country. Under the new constitution, suspects cannot be arrested without due process of the law.

In July 2009 changes were made to Niger's constitution to allow President Mamadou Tandja to remain in office. These were met with protests from some parts of Nigerien society.

Soldiers keeping watch outside a building in Niamey.

THE MILITARY

Niger's armed forces consist of four branches: the army, air force, national police (National Gendarmerie), and the republican guard. The National Gendarmarie is the national paramilitary police force of Niger whose purpose is to provide police protection outside of urban areas. As a landlocked country, Niger does not have a navy. There are 12,000 active duty personnel and 5,000 reservists in total. Military expenditure totals 1.3 percent of gross domestic product (GDP).

Most of Niger's military equipment comes from France, with which it has bilateral defense agreements. Nigeriens between the ages of 17 and 21 can serve two years of voluntary military service. Although peace accords between the government and leaders of the Tuareg have included the integration of the Tuareg fighters into the military forces, the Nigerien armed forces have been fighting an ongoing insurgency in the north of the country, known as the Second Tuareg Rebellion. As of July 2008 up to 160 Nigerien troops had died in the conflict.

PRESIDENT MAMADOU TANDJA

Mamadou Tandja has been the president of Niger since 1999. A popular grassroots politician, he was born in 1938 in the village of Maine Soroa, 870 miles (1,400 km) east of the capital, Niamey. As he was raised in a family of shepherds, he shares natural ties with the rural people of Niger. President Tandja's ancestry is a mixture of both Fulani and Kanouri. He is the first president who does not belong to the Hausa or Djerma ethnic group. He has two wives and is the father of many children.

He is well-liked for his caring attitude to the people of Niger, in particular the rural community. He is widely respected for his sense of pragmatism and justice.

In 1974 he took part in Niger's first military coup, ousting President Hamani Diori. From 1991 to 1999, before he came to power, Tandja served as president of the MNSD. Having unsuccessfully run as the MNSD's presidential candidate in 1993 and 1996, Tandja first came to power in December 1999. He was successfully reelected in 2004, the only time a president of Niger has served two consecutive terms. Tandja has served as an army colonel, interior minister, and an ambassador. He also served as chairman of the Economic Community of West African States from 2005 to 2007.

Since 2005 President Tandja's government has experienced many crises, including severe food shortages due to locust attacks and poor rainfall. Accused of widespread corruption, his government has had to deal with large-scale protests organized by civil society groups and opposition parties. In spite of these problems, he won a victory in August 2009, which allowed him to change the limit on presidential terms of office in the constitution, giving him the right to retain power for an extra three years. President Tandja's motto was "to reconcile Niger's people with work." He himself works hard for his country, and his achievements include the construction of Niger's first oil refinery, the construction of a dam on the Niger River, and the mining of new uranium sites. All these projects have already begun to improve living standards in one of the world's poorest countries.

Tensions grew, however, when he changed the constitution to allow himself to stay in power beyond the legal term limit. This eventually led to the 2010 military coup d'état where rebel soldiers attacked and deposed him, establishing a military junta called the Supreme Council for the Restoration of Democracy (CSRD) in hopes of a more democratic government.

THE FIRST MULTIPARTY ELECTIONS

As the first multiparty legislative elections since independence, the 1993 elections saw the participation of nine political parties. The MNSD, once the sole political Nigerien party, lost the election to a broad alliance of parties. Mahamane Ousmane, who belonged to the Social and Democratic Convention (CDS), became the first freely elected president of Niger.

The Ousmane presidency was marked by student and civil strikes and the continuing Tuareg revolt in the north. In 1995 when President Ousmane failed to accommodate the numerous political groups in the National Assembly, he called for new parliamentary elections. His party, the MNSD, won a slight majority, gaining 29 seats, while the CDS won 24 seats. A coalition government was formed. However, disagreements—mainly over the austerity measures set by the International Monetary Fund—developed between President Ousmane and Prime Minister Hama Amadou, paralyzing the government. Army chief Ibrahim Baré Maïnassara stepped in and overthrew Ousmane, ending Niger's first democratic government. Presidential elections were held in July 1996, which were won by Maïnassara.

Nigeriens at a 2004 Niger Party for Democracy and Socialism rally in Niamey.

Born in May 1949 in Maradi, the son of a schoolteacher, Maïnassara joined the military when he was 21 years old. After attending the Antsérabé Academy in Madagascar, he rose through the ranks. He took part in the 1974 coup when Kountché overthrew Niger's first president, Diori Hamani, and became an aide to Kountché at the age of 25. He attended the military school of infantry in Montpellier, France, for a year and was named chief of the presidential guard in 1976.

After the 1993 elections President Mahamane Ousmane made him chief of staff. After attending the French Interarm Defense College, he was appointed the Nigerien army chief of staff in 1995. He seized power in 1996, putting an end to the democratically elected but politically ineffective presidency of Ousmane.

But his rule was short-lived. On April 9, 1999, Maïnassara was about to board a helicopter at the airport in Niamey when he was assassinated by a group of 12 officers. His death was declared an "unfortunate accident" by Nigerien officials. However, many Nigeriens believe the events surrounding his death are more suspicious. There were, in fact, rumors that he was attempting to flee the country when he was shot down. Maïnassara was succeeded by coup leader Daouda Malam Wanké as head of state. In June 1999 an investigation into his death was started but ended unresolved in September 1999, following an amnesty for coup participants. His party, the RDP-Jama'a, has been demanding an international inquiry into his death.

When Maïnassara was later assassinated, a National Reconciliation Council was formed, and a squadron commander, Daouda Malam Wanké, was named its president and head of the Nigerien state. He promised a referendum vote on the constitution and elections in late 1999. The elections did take place on November 24, 1999, just seven months after the death of Mainassara. The MNSD-Nassara, together with the CDS-Rahama, won the majority of votes and formed the first parliament of the Nigerien Fifth Republic.

POLITICAL PARTIES

NIGERIEN PROGRESSIVE PARTY Formed during the 1946 administrative reforms, the PPN was established in the aftermath of declining interest in the African Democratic Rally (RDA), which was supported by labor unions. Under the leadership of Hamani Diori and with the help of the French administration, it was established as the sole political party when the country gained its independence. In the October 1970 presidential and legislative elections, Diori won 99.98 percent of the vote, while the PPN won a 97.09 percent majority. His government was dissolved in 1974 when it was overthrown by the military. Diori was imprisoned until 1980. In December 2004 the PPN contested the legislative elections in an alliance with the Nigerien Party for Democracy and Socialism.

Hamani Diori,
president of the
Republic of Niger,
in 1965.

NATIONAL MOVEMENT FOR THE DEVELOPMENT OF SOCIETY
Formed in 1988 by General Seybou, who had succeeded Kountché, the MNSD was the sole political party in Niger until 1991. Faced with overwhelming calls for multiparty democracy, and a general strike lasting two days, the ruling party allowed Niger to have its first multiparty parliamentary and presidential elections. An interim government, headed by Amadou Cheiffou, was formed to help the government prepare for the multiparty elections. However, the MNSD failed to gain followers among the Nigerien population. As a result of student and union protests and the Tuareg revolt, the MNSD was forced to accept the establishment of at least 15 other parties. It lost the parliamentary and presidential elections in 1993 when a coalition of nine major opposition parties joined ranks and won control of the parliament and the presidency. In 1995 the MNSD won a majority in parliament when President Ousmane called for early parliamentary elections. In 1999 the party won a major victory, where party member Mamadou Tandja was elected president but was later deposed during the February 2010 military coup d'état.

THE DEMOCARTIC AND SOCIAL CONVENTION OR CDS-RAHAMA

CDS-Rahama was founded in January 1991. Its leader, Mahamane Ousmane, was elected president in 1993. He served until he was ousted in a coup in January 1996. Since 1999 the CDS-Rahama has been in an alliance with the MNSD government, and Ousmane has served as the president of the National Assembly. In 2009, following President Tandja's decision to dismiss the National Assembly and carry out his plans to hold a constitutional referendum on removing limits to the presidential term, CDS-Rahama made a bold decision to separate from the governing MNSD party. As a further sign of protest, the party withdrew its eight members from the Nigerien Council of Ministers. CDS-Rahama demanded that President Tandja submit to the court's negative ruling against the referendum. Recently the party announced the formation of its own opposition coalition, the MDD.

Head of the MNSD-Nassara party Hama Amadou (*left*) sits with the head of the CDS-Rahama party, Mahamane Ousmane (*in blue at the center*).

ECONOMY

Workers at the Tegida salt pan in Niger. Salt is a natural resource extracted in the deserts of Niger, and a good source of income for the Nigeriens.

CHAPTER 4

AS AN ARID AND LANDLOCKED land, Niger can barely sustain its rapidly growing population and its agriculture-based economy. In some areas recurring droughts create serious food shortages for the population and their livestock, and imports have to be brought in to make up for the shortfall.

Niger shares a common currency, the Communaute Financière Africaine franc (CFAF), and a common central bank, the Central Bank of West African States (BCEAO), with seven other members of the West African Monetary Union. In 1994 Niger was able to be more competitive following

According to the United Nations Human Develop-ment Index, Niger ranks as one of the poorest coun-tries in the world. Niger's economy is based largely on some of the world's largest uranium depos-its, livestock, and subsistence crops grown by farmers mainly to feed their fami-lies and their own animals.

A Tuareg woman milking her goat.

the devaluation of its currency. However, this relative prosperity was short-lived. By January 2000 Niger was experiencing serious financial and economic problems. It was forced to seek debt relief assistance from the International Monetary Fund. The crucial debt relief enabled Niger to continue spending on basic areas such as health care, education, and the prevention of poverty.

The discovery of a substantial deposit of uranium at Arlit in the 1960s has significantly boosted Niger's revenues. In the early 1980s, however, a worldwide oversupply of uranium and falling prices forced Niger to tighten its budget. In 2007, as a result of higher world prices, Niger is once again receiving large revenues from its uranium exports. The Nigerien government has recently signed a contract with an American public utilities company to supply 300 (metric) tons of uranium for the next 10 years. In 2008 the real GDP growth rate was at 5.9 percent.

AGRICULTURE

More than 90 percent of the Nigerien population is engaged in agriculture and in raising livestock. Crops are grown mainly in the south where rainfall is

An open-pit uranium mine near Arlit in Niger.

more abundant and the soils are richer. The dry north and Sahel areas, which receive only seasonal rainfall, are used for nomadic stock-raising. Successive droughts in 1971, 1984, and more recently in 2004 to 2005, considerably reduced the size of the cattle herds.

Groundnuts, or peanuts—the most important cash crop in Niger—are planted in the sandy soils of Maradi and Zinder. Niger is the third-largest peanut grower in Africa. Cowpeas and onions are grown for commercial export, as are limited quantities of garlic, pepper, gum arabic, and sesame seeds. To diversify the economy and reduce Niger's dependence on peanuts, cotton was introduced as a crop in 1956. It is cultivated in the Tahoua region. Niger's main food crops are sorghum and millet, which are grown on about 90 percent of the cultivated land. Millet is usually grown by itself in light soil, but sometimes it is planted among rows of peanuts or beans. Sorghum requires a richer soil than millet. A small portion of the millet and sorghum production is exported. Since 1980 there has been an increased interest in vegetables and grains as cash crops.

Niger imports grains, including wheat, rice, corn, millet, and sorghum. The harvest varies as much as 10 percent from year to year, depending on the amount of rainfall—production can fall by as much as 40 percent during the drought years and, correspondingly, it can yield more in the good rainfall years. Most of the rice produced is consumed locally. As demand for cassava and beans increases, cultivation of these crops has grown. Nigeriens also grow tomatoes, wheat, and sugarcane. Most of the sugarcane plantations are located near Tillabéry. Wheat is grown in Agadez, near Lake Chad, and in the Aïr and Kuwar mountains. Tomatoes grow well in Tahoua, Zinder, and Agadez.

Workers taking a rest at a local plantation.

HUSBANDRY AND FISHING

Husbandry is Niger's most important activity. Land that is unsuitable for agriculture is used for grazing animals. Herds traditionally move north during the rainy season. The animals are the herders' capital and only resource. Used for transportation, the animals also provide milk, meat, and leather. The leather is used for the awnings of tents, clothes, shoes, and ropes. In a good year, communities can perform social and religious activities, such as making donations, and making sacrifices.

The main herd animal is zebu, a member of the ox family that is characterized by curved horns shaped like a harp and a relatively large, fleshy hump over its shoulders. The zebu has pendulous ears and a distinct resistance to heat and insect attacks. Other herd animals include goats, sheep, and camels. Fishing activities are limited to areas along the banks of the Niger River and near Lake Chad.

A busy livestock market. The size of the herds has improved significantly since the drought years, and demand has increased.

MINING AND INDUSTRY

In 1960 Niger started a program to develop its mineral resources. As a result, uranium was discovered at Arlit in the Agadez region in 1967. Huge coal reserves were also discovered northeast of Agadez. Today the uranium sector provides Niger with approximately 55.4 percent of national export proceeds. After the discovery of uranium in the 1960s, Niger enjoyed large export earnings that significantly benefited its economy. Money was channeled to the development of infrastructure, industry, communications, and training. However, in the early 1980s, the oversupply and falling prices of uranium adversely affected the economy. Since 2007, as a result of higher prices, Niger is again earning large sums for its uranium. In 2007 the government of Niger awarded 122 new mineral exploration licenses to companies from France, China, Canada, Australia, India, South Africa, and the United States.

Bottling drinks in a factory. These industrial companies are usually of a modest size, not large-scale enterprises.

The main buyer of Niger's uranium is France. Besides mining in the north, Niger's industrial production includes a manufacturing industry in the south, where factories process agricultural products, such as peanuts, millet, sorghum, cotton, and cattle products. Smaller industrial units focus on making cement and mortar bricks for local consumption. Recently deposits of gold have also been found in Niger, in the region between the Niger River and the border with Burkina Faso. In 2004 President Tandja announced the official opening of the Samira Hill Gold Mine, the first commercial gold production facility, in the region of Tera. Significant deposits of phosphates, iron, limestone, and gypsum have also been found in Niger.

TRANSPORTATION

Because it has no railroads or ports, Niger relies on roads for transportation. Niger's road grid includes east-to-west and north-to-south roads that provide

A heavily loaded truck crossing the Sahara desert. Because Niger is a landlocked country, trucks and other forms of land transportation are especially useful for Nigeriens.

access to neighboring countries. The main roads include those from Niamey to Zinder, Tahoua, Arlit, and Gaya. Many other roads may only be traveled after gaining special permission from the government of Niger. Many secondary roads are made of dirt and gravel, which can be impassable after heavy rains. The total length of highways is 11,526 miles (14,565 km), of which only 2,363 miles (3,641 km) are paved.

Niger has two international airports: Diori Hamani International Airport, serving Niamey; and Mano Dayak International Airport, serving the city of Agadez. Niger is not well served by international connections. The only direct European connection is offered by Air France from Paris to Niamey or Agadez. Other than that, it is only possible to access the country via regional and neighboring capitals. Afriqiyah Airways flies directly to Niamey from Tripoli, Air Algérie from Algiers, Air Burkina from Ouagadougou, and Royal Air Maroc from Casablanca.

The national airline, Air Niger, offers domestic air services between Diffa, Tillabéry, Zinder, and Arlit. To transport goods overseas, Niger uses the Cotonou port in Benin and the Lagos port in Nigeria.

Between December and March, the Niger River is navigable for 186 miles (299 km) from Niamey to Gaya, which lies on the border with Benin. Canoes are used to ferry people across rivers. In the rural areas, where road networks are less developed, donkeys and camels are used. It is not unusual to see camels crossing the bridges in the capital city of Niamey.

OTHER RESOURCES

Niger has a huge oil potential. Its largest oil deposit lies at the Agadem block, north of Chad. In June 2007 the China National Petroleum Corporation signed a $5 billion agreement to extract oil in the Agadem block, as well as to build an oil refinery and an oil pipeline.

AZALAY, THE 2,500-YEAR-OLD SALT CARAVAN

Originating in the fifth century B.C.*, the azalay (ah-ZAH-lay) is an ancient system of transportation that refers to a caravan of camels that travels a large distance. Today these legendary caravans still ply the Ténéré Desert and link Agadez to the oases of Bilma and Fachi, which provide salt, dates, and natron. The much-sought-after natron, a low-grade carbonate of soda found in the oases of Kawar, is consumed by both humans and animals.*

Crossing the Ténéré takes about three weeks. The caravans can consist of 10,000 to 20,000 camels and can stretch for 16 miles (26 km). Traveling over vast distances, these caravans often face attacks by bandits. The caravans are mostly manned by the Tuareg, but other ethnic groups, such as the Hausa and Toubou, are also attracted to this way of life.

Mining operations have also discovered copper, lignite, zinc, chromium, molybdenum, tungsten, lithium, and titanium.

The government has built a hydroelectric power station and a coal-burning power station. The Office of Solar Energy is producing solar batteries, which are used to power the country's telecommunications network.

ENVIRONMENT

Camels and goats visit a waterhole surrounded by Doum palms at an oasis in the Sahara desert of Niger.

CHAPTER 5

NIGER, ONE OF THE poorest countries in the world, has experienced extreme drought, food shortages, and increased desertification over the last 30 years, as a result of global climate change and careless use of its scant natural resources. In the mid-2000s Niger suffered terribly from a food crisis, caused by severe droughts.

Families enjoying the convenience of a modern and clean water supply in Niamey. A supply of good drinking water is a challenge for more than half the Nigerien population, who have to go directly to rivers or natural storm water reserves, which are often dirty.

The vast landlocked country of Niger faces increasing demands upon its scarce resources, which has resulted in high levels of death and disease among its people throughout the nation's history. Looking after the environment of Niger and its land is paramount, as a large proportion of the population depends on the land for their subsistence. In fact 90 percent of the population relies on the land, although only 12 percent of the land can be cultivated. Many people in Niger subsist on less than a dollar a day, making their living from traditional farming and livestock-rearing in this harsh and uncompromising climate.

Recurring drought, coupled with lack of rainfall and a growing population, has placed severe pressure on the environment. Living in this fragile environment, many people in Niger feel as though they are never far from disaster and extreme poverty.

Besides the main concerns of desertification and drought, Niger's other environmental issues today include overgrazing, soil erosion, deforestation, and threats to its wildlife population. The government has demonstrated its commitment by increased investment in the national budget to be spent on useful projects to help the environment. It is evident that the government and other politicians take Niger's environmental concerns very seriously as the recent elections have been fought over these pressing and current environmental issues.

DESERTIFICATION

As in many parts of the world, desertification has posed a threat to the Sahel. The desert already occupies over 80 percent of Niger. But in the 1990s it was reported that 965 square miles (2,500 square km) of land were being lost each year in Niger through desertification.

A drought in Niger leaves these cows emaciated and near death.

Desertification is caused mainly by the reckless use of land—for example, overgrazing and slash-and-burn techniques in agriculture. About 100 years ago the farmers in the Sahel did farm the land, but their agricultural practices were balanced out by hunting activities. They were able to feed their families by hunting for lions, elephants, giraffes, ostriches, addax, antelopes, and deer for meat and hides. In colonial times farmers in the south of Niger were actively encouraged to cultivate land commercially to produce peanuts for export. The growth of the peanut industry has resulted in the rapid destruction of stable perennial vegetation. This, in turn, has caused widespread desertification. Today farmers rely solely on agriculture for their livelihoods. In the Sahel farmers have used brutal slash-and-burn methods to clear natural forests and bushland for agricultural use. The destruction of the vegetation causes the land to be exposed and soil erosion to occur, leaving the land barren and infertile. Fortunately for the large percentage of Nigeriens who rely on agriculture for survival, there is a natural greenbelt situated north of the town of Tânout that protects the farmers from the Sahara Desert. This area is rich with perennials and even wildlife such as gazelles and desert partridges. The flora and fauna offer protection to the area by fending off wind and water erosion.

Crops being harvested in Niger.

In spite of the fact that parts of Niger have already suffered greatly from the negative effects of desertification, researchers were surprised and impressed to discover that, since the mid-2000s, the situation has improved dramatically. In some areas farmers have even managed to halt the process of desertification almost completely. Simply by implementing basic preventative techniques such as planting trees and preserving natural vegetation, approximately 11.6 million square miles (30 million square km) of severely degraded land has been successfully rehabilitated, according to the Nigerien government. As a result of massive tree-planting programs, there is an abundance of new trees in certain parts of southern Niger—up to 20 times more trees in 2005 than 30 years earlier. These antidesertification programs are good news for the environment as well as for the economy, as tens of thousands of people will gain employment to carry out the work of replanting and reforesting. In 2006 the government pledged a total of 1.25 billion XOF ($2.8 million in U.S. dollars) each year to tackle the problems of desertification, including restoring damaged lands, sand dunes, and oasis water. Niger's success at restoring its environment

A acacia tree nursery in Niger, where the saplings are carefully tended prior to transplanting.

against desertification is an encouraging model for what can be achieved by simple means combined with government support. Niger's reforestation programs have the full backing of the government.

An onion field in Niger.

It is impressive that, through the efforts made in its antidesertification programs, Niger now has the problem of desertification under control and is carrying out further improvements for the future. Niger's farmers are delighted with the results, as this means they can once again make a living from the land and be independent. This can be clearly seen by the vast increase in the production of one of Niger's most important cash crops, the onion. In 2005, it was reported that, in the last 20 years, onion production has tripled to 297,624 tons (270,000 metric tons), which are exported mainly to Nigeria and Benin. Combating the effects of desertification has enhanced the quality of life for farmers and their families in Niger. A few of the more important benefits can be seen in the decrease in child mortality and the ability of some farmers to send their children to school to receive an education. However, these improvements may be short-lived if the birthrate continues to increase at its current explosive rate. It is estimated that Niger's population will rise to 56 million by 2050, compared with 13 million in 2008. Experts are also quick to offer reminders that Niger still suffers from other environmental issues, which contributes to its food crisis, including climate change, erratic rainfall, and soil degradation.

Today parts of Niger are enjoying more pockets of greenery than they have ever had in its history. In the Sahel and other parts of southern Niger, reforestation projects, including the Farmer Managed Natural Regeneration (FMNR) reforestation technique, were established in the mid-1980s to replant millions of trees. FMNR is a simple technique, promoted in hundreds of villages across Niger, whereby indigenous tree and shrub stumps are selected and their stronger stems carefully pruned to allow more sprouts to grow. It has been found that, under this FMNR method, up to 20 stems may sprout from a single stump.

Farmers have played an essential and effective role by revegetating their own once-barren wasteland while they are in the process of cultivating. Newly planted trees help the land retain nutrients, including precious soil and water. These tree-planting programs, combined with enhanced rainfall levels, have resulted in approximately 7 million acres (1.1 million square km) of land that are now flourishing with invaluable clumps of new trees. Best of all, not only is tree-planting a highly effective way of restoring fertility to previously degraded land, but it also costs farmers very little. About 20 years ago farmers in the Sahel noticed that their trees were disappearing into the distance and once fertile land was being lost to the already vast desert. What they saw frightened them so much that independent groups of farmers decided to protect young trees and saplings instead of destroying them. Instead of clearing them away or cutting down trees for wood, the farmers would plant their crops around them.

Farmers also began to realize that they could make money from parts of their trees, for example, by selling fruit and seeds for food and even bark and branches for construction purposes. They also saw that certain trees were essential to agriculture. For instance, the nitrogen produced by the gao tree and its fallen leaves help fertilize the soil around it. Today farmers and their communities are reaping the benefits of their wise actions. The replanting of trees has enabled them to restore the land, grow crops for food, and become profitable once again. The reclamation of the land through the regrowing of trees has benefited the rural communities of Niger enormously. In the village of Dansaga, for instance, the replanting of trees has meant that many lives were saved in the food crisis in 2005, mainly as a result of the earnings gained from selling wood from the trees. In some villages trees have become so valuable that poachers are cutting them down without permission to sell for profit (below). Farmers have found that it has been difficult to take legal action against these poachers and their crimes. Still it is encouraging to see that, based on a simple idea of protecting and replanting trees, it is possible to alleviate the sufferings of the poor in Niger.

Thousands of women and children lined up to receive aid at a food distribution center in the village of Yama in northwestern Niger during the 2005 food crisis.

CLIMATE CHANGE, DROUGHT, AND FOOD CRISIS

It has been estimated by the UK-based charity OXFAM that severe food shortages could affect up to 60 million Africans by the 2080s. According to a United Nations (UN) survey done in 2005, almost 12 percent of children in Niger under the age of five suffer from malnutrition. Desertification is only one of the factors that have contributed to poor harvests and food shortages in Niger and the rest of Africa. In the last decade, climatic changes, severe droughts, and erratic rainfall levels have been significant factors contributing to the hunger crisis. In 2005 a drop in precipitation caused Niger to suffer its worst-ever food crisis.

Today, although rainfall levels are improving, scientists have stated that the rains have not completely recovered, as compared with rainfall levels recorded in the 1950s. It is believed that Niger will continue to be fragile, and its people will be exposed to drought and hunger. Scientific predictions indicate that there will, in fact, be less rainfall in the Sahel in the long term, caused by rising temperatures in the Gulf of Guinea. In an attempt to make the country less vulnerable, Niger, together with other poor African countries, has joined large-scale water, sanitation, and hygiene promotion projects established in 2007 by the International Federation of Red Cross and Red Cresent Societies' Global Water and Sanitation Initiative. These projects aim to use basic technologies to educate communities on how to maintain and operate their water supplies economically. There is also a push to promote personal hygiene by building latrines in schools and encouraging children to use them. These actions, if successful, will gradually reduce the threat of cholera and other diseases, especially in times of drought and hunger.

THE 2005 FOOD CRISIS

The Niger food crisis of 2005 mainly affected the regions of northern Maradi, Tahoua, Tillaberi, and Zinder. Several factors contributed to making this the country's worst food crisis yet—an unexpected and premature termination to the rains in 2004, a fierce attack by desert locusts causing damage to some pasture lands, increasing food prices, and chronic poverty. Up to 3.6 million adults and 150,000 children faced acute food shortage, hunger, and, in some cases, even starvation. Although it was severe, the food crisis did not come as a surprise to the authorities.

In 2004 inadequate rainfall had resulted in a poor harvest that was mainly destroyed by waves of locusts. It is estimated that, in certain areas, 100 percent of the harvest was destroyed. This caused a sharp rise—up to 20 percent—in food prices and other basic goods, which made the situation unbearable for many people who were already experiencing extreme hunger. Although the government offered subsidies, the impoverished farmers were still unable to afford to buy food for their families. The lack of food and water affected people as well as their animals, such as cattle, camels, sheep, and goats. The ill health and sometimes death of these animals, which in themselves are an important source of food, made the food crisis even more severe.

In February 2005 the United Nations established an emergency food program to help thousands of starving people, but sadly, international aid was slow and failed to reach many needy people. Hundreds of Nigeriens attempted to escape the food crisis by crossing over the border to Nigeria. Others marched in the capital of Niamey to demand free food. According to the World Health Organization (WHO), by mid-2005, an estimated 800,000 children under the age of five were suffering from a degree of malnutrition. Of these at least 160,000 were malnourished and 32,000 were severely malnourished. Even today the children of Niger are suffering from the effects of malnutrition and disease.

THREATS TO WILDLIFE

As in many other African countries, Niger's wildlife population is under real threat mainly because of the illegal practice of poaching and the destruction of natural habitats. Animals that are endangered in Niger today include giraffes, elephants, hippopotami, lions, and some others. In January 2001 Niger introduced a hunting ban in an effort to save its wildlife population.

One of the animals facing critical threat is the addax. According to the Sahara Conservation Fund, there are only about 200 addax remaining in the deserts of Niger today. The addax inhabits the regions of Termit and Tin Toumma in the Sahara. This region is rich with other desert wildlife, including bustards and tortoises, gazelles, Barbary sheep, cheetahs, striped hyenas, fennecs, Rüppell's foxes, pale foxes, sand cats, wildcats, golden jackals, and vultures, just to name a few. Conservationists are working hard to ensure the survival of the addax in this unique and beautiful region. In the past wildlife flourished in this isolated region. In recent years, however, the oil industry has encroached on this region and has begun to construct camps and airstrips. There are plans to build oil refineries and pipelines where drilling will take place in the heart of this peaceful desert. Fortunately the Sahara Conservation Fund is helping the Niger government establish a new 39,000-square-mile (101,010-square-km) Termit-Tin Toumma National Nature Reserve, specifically for the region's critically endangered wildlife. By establishing boundaries and mapping and surveying the wildlife population, it is hoped that all wildlife, including the addax, will continue to survive and flourish.

Apart from the threat from the oil industry, the wildlife population is also challenged by the practice of illegal poaching. In these parts, gazelle poaching is popular. One animal that is already extinct in Niger is the scimitar-horned oryx, which is a large antelope with long, backward-sweeping, curved horns. They were probably last seen in Niger in the 1990s. Up to the late 1970s there were several thousand of them, but today, they are extinct in the wild. It is believed that their extinction has been caused by a mixture of factors, including poaching, drought, desertification, and the destruction of their natural habitat by agriculture. It is possible, however, to see the scimitar-horned oryx in zoos across the world.

Niger's major national park is the "W" National Park. The park was so named because the Niger River, which meanders through it, is shaped like the letter "W." The "W" National Park was created in 1954 and declared a UNESCO World Heritage Site in 1996. This national park covers a massive area of about 5,406.9 square miles (14,003.8 square km), taking in three countries, including Niger, Benin, and Burkina Faso. Historically the park has been inhabited by both humans and wildlife. The park is home to aardvarks, baboons, buffalo, caracals, cheetahs, elephants, hippopotami, leopards, lions, servals, and warthogs. Approximately 350 species of birds can be found here.

A leopard relaxes at the "W" National Park in Niger.

NIGERIENS

A female Tuareg warrior and guardian of the Sultan of Agadez. This is an inherited position in the matrilineal Tuareg culture.

LANGUAGES DISTINGUISH THE people of Niger, who can be categorized into five language groups: the Hausa, the Djerma-Songhai, the Fulani, the Tuareg, and the Kanouri.

The Hausa make up about 55 percent of the population, while the Djerma-Songhai form 21 percent. The Peuhl are 8.5 percent of the population, the Tuareg 9 percent, and the Kanouri 4.7 percent. Smaller groups include the Toubou, Arabs, and Gourmantché, which together constitute about 1.2 percent. There are several thousand French expatriates in Niger.

In Niger, most Muslims are Sunni Muslims. Most Nigeriens use the Hausa language in trade and in everyday life. Most of the country's ethnic groups maintain close relationships with their relatives in neighboring countries such as Chad and Nigeria.

Peuhl bachelors during the *Gerewol* ceremony. Bororo women, who are watching the men dance, will remove their brass trinkets after conceiving their second child.

A typical Hausa village in Niger.

THE HAUSA

The Hausa make up about 55 percent of the Nigerien population. The Hausa are also present in northern Niger, where they dominate Nigerien economic and political life. There are about 30 to 35 million Hausa people in West Africa. Some of their ancestors can be traced back to the Sokoto Empire, an Islamic confederation that was based in northern Nigeria in the 19th century. The Hausa live in the mid-south region of Niger, where the population density is the highest in the country. Their area extends past the city of Filingué in the west, Zinder in the east, and from Tahoua to Niger's border with Nigeria. A small number can also be found as far north as the Aïr region.

Although most Nigerien Hausa are farmers, they are also acknowledged as astute businesspeople. They have created an economy based on grain food crops, livestock, cash crops such as peanuts and cotton, and craft production. There are many excellent Hausa artisans in Niger, famous for their elaborate leatherwork. Because of mobility and extensive business contacts the language of the Hausa is understood and widely spoken by more than half of the population. Despite a common language and distinctive cultural heritage, the Hausa consists of subgroups with their own states. They include the Arawa, Adarawa, Gobirawa, Katsinwa, Dorawa, Damagarawa, Tazarawa, Kouannawa, Kurfayawa, Damargawa, and Cangawa.

Muslim Hausa society is characterized by a complex system of rank based on profession, wealth, and birth. Occupational specializations are often passed down from father to son.

A group of Songhai women enjoy socializing together.

THE SONGHAI-DJERMA

The Songhai and Djerma are different peoples who speak the same language. Because they share a common culture, other groups view them as one people. They are distinguished from each other by a slight difference in their local dialects and the theory of their origins before the 18th century. Forming almost 21 percent of the total population, the Songhai-Djerma are sedentary people who farm in the western part of the country near the Niger River. Apart from the late President Maïnassara, the first Hausa president of Niger, political power has remained in the hands of the Songhai-Djerma since Niger's independence.

The Djerma population is twice as large as the Songhai. They mainly live on the left bank of the Niger River, around the city of Dosso. Other Djerma live in Mali and Benin. Although their origin is still a question, they are known for their fighting agility and have helped their cousins, the Songhai, in numerous battles against the Tuareg and the Fulani.

The Songhai live on the right bank of the Niger River and in the Ayorou-Tillabéry region on the left bank. They can also be found in Mali, Benin, and Burkina Faso. The Songhai are descendants of the 15th-century Songhai Empire.

THE PEUHL

The nomadic Peuhl or Fulani are scattered all over the Sahel and live in almost all of Niger, except in the northeast oases. They also live in Nigeria, Cameroon, and other African countries. *Peul* is a French word used by the French colonists. Numbering about 25 million in West Africa, they are of mixed African origins. They were also recorded as the first people to settle in the Senegambia region.

Two Peuhl girls in southwestern Niger dress up in their finest clothing and jewelry to attend the weekly market in Torodi.

Since the last century, many Peuhl have settled in the south. Most of them are engaged in agriculture. Others lead scholarly Islamic lifestyles, while the rest are nomads in the north. Migrations to urban or semiurban regions have been getting more common in recent years due to unpredictable crop harvests. Although the Peuhl are the third-largest group in Niger, forming about 8.5 percent of the total Nigerien population, they are not a majority in any region. The 25 million Fulani in West Africa constitute the second-largest ethnic group in the region, second only to the Hausa.

The Peuhl, who speak Fulfuldé, are dispersed in various West African countries from Senegal to Chad. The close similarity of their language to the native language of Senegal indicates a possible origin in this West African country. It is believed that after adopting a new language in Senegal, they spread eastward by the 10th century and reached Nigeria by the 14th century.

In the late 18th century, a dispute developed between the Peuhl and a Hausa sultan over the imprisonment of the followers of a Peuhl cleric, Uthman dan Fodio. A holy war was declared in 1810 and was won by the Peuhl. Under the rule of Uthman, the vast Peuhl empire was created and administered strictly according to Koranic law. The Peuhl even established several kingdoms in Senegal and Cameroon. Uthman was succeeded by his son Muhammed Bello in 1815 who built the city of Sokoto. In the late 19th century the British begun to penetrate the empire and successfully defeated the Peuhl by the early 20th century.

Within the Peuhl the Bororo form a distinct subgroup, holding tightly to their ancient traditions. The Bororo live in the Dakoro-Tânout region. Most have preserved their animist beliefs, although some have converted to Islam. As lovers of beauty, they hold an annual Gerewol (GER-e-wol) festival, a beauty contest for unmarried men. Although Bororo women pay great attention to their appearance, it is mainly the Bororo men who embellish themselves. Popular accessories include earrings, coins woven into an elaborate hairstyle, bead necklaces, and multicolored charms.

A Peuhl family.

THE KANOURI

The Hausa refer to the Kanouri as Beriberi. The Kanouri live east of the Hausa region and on the western side of Lake Chad, the site of the Kanem-Bornu Empire. Like the Hausa and the Djerma-Songhai, the Kanouri are mainly farmers. They specialize in the preparation of salt, and many of them are excellent fishermen. Some are cattle herders. Through mixed marriages, they have blended with other groups. They have particularly close ties with Hausa speakers.

The Kanouri are divided into subgroups: the Manga, the Dagora, the Mober, the Buduma, and the Kanumba. Besides Niger, the Kanouri also live in Chad, Cameroon, and Nigeria.

THE TUAREG

The Tuareg settled in the Aïr region as early as the seventh century, expanding their territory gradually to the entire Sahara region. Known as desert warriors, the Tuareg are famous for their fighting skills. Today they are found in the Algerian, Nigerien, Malian, and Libyan portions of the Sahara, where they form about eight major groups.

Jewelry is an important feature in the attire of the Tuareg women.

In the past, the Tuareg operated the trans-Saharan caravan trade and were known to capture prisoners for trade or for use as laborers. Today the Tuareg lead a nomadic life, although the droughts in the past decades have forced some to live permanently in cities such as Agadez.

The Tuareg are divided into three major subgroups: the Kel Aïr, the Kel Azawak, and the Kel Geres. The Kel Aïr live in the Aïr region and the Damergou region. Most of them are gardeners and shopkeepers. Most of the Kel Azawak are nomads, although a few animal herders can sometimes be found. The Kel Geres are herders and farmers.

Tuareg society, unlike most Muslim societies, is matrilineal, and women have a prominent role. In contrast to the women in many Arab and Muslim societies, Tuareg women are neither veiled nor secluded. Camp life is the Tuareg woman's domain, and she can own herds of animals and slaves. Women own the family property and manage the finances. They also play musical instruments and participate in organized musical performances.

The light-skinned Tuareg men are sometimes called "blue men." Except for their eyes, they wrap their entire body in indigo-dyed clothes to protect themselves from the sandy winds and scorching sun, and the blue color rubs off onto their faces. At the end of the day, the men usually gather for their favorite pastime—the ceremonial sipping of tea next to a fire and talking about journeys in the desert.

One feature that has made the Tuareg an object of curiosity is the headdress and veil, worn by all adult Tuareg males. Despite its style variations, the basic veil, called the tagelmust *(tag-ERL-moost)*, is a large piece of Sudanese cotton, measuring 59 to 158 inches (150—401 cm) long by 10 to 20 inches (25—50 cm) wide. It can be made of several strips of cotton that the Tuareg wrap around the head to form a low turban. The veil rests on the nose and falls on the face down to the upper part of the chest. Only the eyes are revealed.

Once a Tuareg boy enters puberty, he wears the veil in a family ceremony that marks his passage from adolescence to adulthood. From then on, he rarely goes unveiled, wearing the veil even while he is sleeping. The fold above the nose is frequently and slightly adjusted when he is in a group.

Although veiling is an ancient custom, its origins remain obscure. The veil holds an important place in Tuareg society, because it is a symbolic manifestation of the role status in Tuareg groups: The lower the veil is worn, the higher one's status.

A group of Toubou travelers with their camel caravans.

THE TOUBOU

A small number of Toubou live in dispersed settlements in areas north of Gouré, up to the Djado Plateau region. This tiny minority originated in the rocky region of Tibesti in Chad, where they number more than 350,000. There are also approximately several thousand Toubou people living in Libya and Nigeria.

The Toubou are known for their quest for adventure and achievement and their love of war and guns. As highly independent individuals, they are divided into the Kesherda and the Wandalas. The Kesherda lead a seminomadic life and are excellent caravan travelers. They are also good cattle herders and hunters. The Wandalas lead sedentary lives—some are farmers mainly cultivating crops such as dates and grains, while others look after livestock.

ETHNIC MINORITIES

Besides the main ethnic groups, the Hausa, Zarma, Tuareg, and Peuhl, there are a number of small groups who live in the Republic of Niger. Some of them work for the main groups, while others form their own settlements. Niger's minorities include the Arabs and the Gourmantché, who are pastoralists. Together with the Toubou, they form about 1.2 percent of the Nigerien population. The Arabs live north of Tahoua and Nguigmi, dress like the Tuareg, and speak their language, whereas the Gourmantché live on the right bank of the Niger River. The other minorities consist of Africans from other countries and a small number of Europeans. A large proportion of Europeans are French, descendants of the French colonists.

The total population of Niger was 15,306,252 in 2009.

WOMEN IN SOCIETY

Many women in Niger live in a patriarchal system dominated by a conservative interpretation of Islam, which have contributed to the exclusion of women from full participation in political and social life. Currently fewer than 7 percent of women are employed in official income-generating activities, compared with 81 percent of men. As in most West African countries, discrimination against girls in education also exists in Niger. The result is a low literacy rate of 15.1 percent among females. The literacy rate of males is almost three times higher, at 42.9 percent.

Nigerien mothers and their children.

Among the women who receive an education, only a few reach high levels of public administration. If they do climb to the top, they encounter serious limitations. For example, in 1991, when educated women demanded a greater role in a national conference, they were met with hostility and physical violence from Islamic leaders. However, things are gradually changing for the better for women in Niger. The December 2004 elections resulted in enormous political gains for women. Out of 113 seats, 14 were won by women, representing 12.4 percent in the National Assembly. This demonstrates a vast improvement in the position of women in Nigerien society where, in the 1995 elections, the legislature only had one female member. Today women politicians hold some important portfolios in foreign affairs, enterprise privatization and redevelopment, employment and public works, and population and social action, to name a few.

In rural areas, women are actively involved in efforts to improve their children's health. Much of their time is spent hauling water, gathering firewood, doing the numerous household chores, and taking care of their offspring. Nigerien women have a high fertility rate, with an average of seven children each.

Local women waiting for training from an active women's group in Niger.

Many women's organizations are working in Niger to enhance the condition of women and their children. For example, UNICEF is working toward empowering women in the region of Maradi to improve child survival and tackle poverty. Representatives visit towns and villages to promote essential family practices such as simple ways to treat diarrhea. Other projects include sessions where mothers and women are taught about the importance of hand washing, complimentary feeding, vaccinations, and hygenic techniques of breast-feeding. Women are also taught how to ask for medical help or advice from health professionals for their children when needed. UNICEF hopes to reach out to a population of 74,000 people living in 51 places in the region of Maradi within a period of three years. In other parts of Niger, groups of women, with the help of women's organizations, are saving money to enable them to start their own small businesses to generate income for their families. Other women's groups working in Niger include the Niger Delta Women for Justice, which aims to support disadvantaged women, particularly those in rural areas and urban slums. The charity CARE also runs training for women's groups in Niger. For example, the charity has worked in the districts of Dosso, Tahoua, and Tillaberi, helping women grow the livestock sector by developing access to credit and training, as well as educating them on ways to market their animal products. All these types of programs help women become more involved and better equipped at caring for their family, which gives them a sense of dignity. To help women who have been victims of domestic abuse, groups such as SOS Children Villages Worldwide, a charity set up in 1993 by the Nigerien government for orphaned and abandoned children, and a consortium of other Nigerien NGOs, are focusing on providing legal and medical assistance to women.

WOMEN IN A MALE-DOMINATED WORLD

In Niger, despite the constitution's provisions for women's rights, the deep-seated traditional belief that women should be subordinate to men results in discrimination in education, employment, and property rights. Women's inferior legal status is revealed, for example, in head of household status—a male head of household has certain legal rights, but divorced or widowed women, even with children, are not considered to be heads of households. Among more conservative Hausa and Peuhl families, women are shut away at home, and some are only allowed to leave their homes if they are escorted by a male member of the family. Tradition among some ethnic groups from rural families allows girls as young as 12 to enter into marriage agreements.

Female genital mutilation, which has been illegal since 2003 and is widely condemned by international health experts as damaging to both physical and psychological health, is still practiced by several ethnic groups in the extreme western and far eastern areas of the country. Domestic violence and physical abuse against women is believed to be common. Women's groups report that prostitution is often seen as the only viable way for a woman to be economically independent.

Human rights experts have reported that 70 percent of women admit that their husbands, fathers, and brothers regularly beat, rape, and humiliate them. Although violence against women is rampant, the subject remains taboo in Nigerien society. In 1999, even though the male-dominated government signed a United Nations antidiscrimination instrument called the Convention for the Elimination of Discrimination against Women, it ensured that reservations were made on key articles to limit a married woman's right to choose her own place of residence and to divorce. However, human rights activists say there is hope as there is a growing awareness among some women of their rights. On November 25, 2007, to mark the international day for eliminating violence against women, hundreds of women bravely turned out for a march in central Niamey.

LIFESTYLE

A Tuareg woman bathing her baby.

CHAPTER 7

MORE THAN 80 PERCENT OF Nigeriens live in rural areas, and their living habits vary according to their group's ethnicity, religion, profession, and residence.

In the rural areas, no one works alone. To ensure survival, everyone has to chip in, in order to reap a bountiful harvest at the end of the agricultural year. Urban centers offer people the opportunity to break away from the limits of ancient traditions, especially for those who come from less-developed areas. The social hierarchy of past empires—nobles, free people, and descendants of slaves—still exists today. It contributes to the interactions of the groups and an individual's profession.

Local women drawing water from a communal well. During the dry season in rural Niger, when the rivers dry up, Nigeriens have to dig deep to find water.

Because many Nigeriens, in both urban and rural areas, live under harsh conditions, a common characteristic of the people is cooperation and solidarity among members of the family and the community at large.

NOMADS

Nomads in Niger include mainly the Tuareg and the Fulani. The harsh and sometimes treacherous desert life requires strong ties between group members. To survive everyone has to cooperate well and work together for the good of the group.

A Tuareg nomadic group usually consists of five noble families, five artisan families, and 15 slave families. When several clans form an alliance, the name of the alliance is prefixed with *Kel*. The largest Tuareg confederation is Kel Owey, which migrated to Niger around the 15th century. The leader of the clan is called *amrar* (AHM-rahr), which means "old." The leader decides on the daily tasks of the camp and allocates activities to the artisans and herders. When a confederation of several clans unites, their leader is called *amenokal* (ah-MEN-noh-kal).

Unlike the Tuareg groups, a less-structured hierarchy exists among the Fulani. When an individual is born, he or she is categorized, based on kinship, age, sex, and generation. These remain important determinants of existence, which the Fulani accept. Another factor that determines a person's status in Fulani society is the number of cattle the person owns and his or her success in rearing them.

Bororo Fulani nomads, who usually move around in groups.

Severe droughts in the 1970s, 1980s, and more recently in 2005 have dealt a heavy blow to the nomads. They gradually lost most of their herds, and the remaining people were forced to take on a sedentary life for which they were not prepared. Many sought refuge in neighboring countries.

TUAREG NOMAD GEAR

To survive in the desert, the Tuareg nomad must have certain necessary utensils and equipment. These include:

1. Taoussit *(TA-oh-seet): A mat to sit or sleep on*
2. Asaber *(ah-SA-ber): A mat used as a windscreen or to create a private space*
3. Aghrik *(ah-GREEK): A leather bag that holds the family's belongings*
4. Abayor *(ah-BAR-yoor): A goatskin, tanned with an acacia bark that holds fresh water. Its shape enables it to be easily carried by animals.*
5. Tagelmust *(tag-ERL-moost): A long turban that men wear on the head and use to cover their face*
6. Alesho *(ah-LEH-sho): Indigo-colored cloth pieces sewn together and worn by the women like a scarf*

Zebu and other cattle being herded.

SOCIAL STRUCTURE

Niger's present population is the result of numerous migrations by different ethnic groups. Social structure generally originated in the days of the trade caravans and wars. Most of these rankings are also prevalent in West Africa. As a result, there is uniformity within the ethnic diversity of Niger. Each ethnic group is organized into family, clan, and confederations and is well adapted to both sedentary and nomadic lifestyles. For example, within the Tuareg community, several family groups make up a clan. A series of clans may unite together under a supreme chief, forming a *Kel* or confederation. (The word *Kel* means "those of.") Tuaregs define themselves according to their specific Kel. For instance, Kel Ahaggar are "those of the Ahaggar Mountains."

In villages the elders, who are also the keepers of oral tradition, maintain social organizations that determine interactions between members of a social group, their social behavior, and interactions with other ethnic groups.

Ancient animist customs (the belief that spirits exist not just in humans but in every object, including animals and plants), coupled with Islamic traditions, continue to define the lives of the majority of the people. Rural lifestyles are now being affected by a rising number of people who are receiving basic education in schools. A greater number of people, especially the educated, are also attracted to the cities.

For over two thousand years, Tuaregs have led a nomadic life, living and traveling across the Sahara Desert. Today, Tuareg people lead a settled lifestyle, seeking employment in the mining areas.

SOCIAL UNITS

In permanent settlements, the basic unit of Nigerien social life is the family. Nigeriens define themselves in terms of patrilineages, with all males and females descending from a single male ancestor. Leaders are usually chosen from the oldest men in a family, and their duties include partitioning and allocating plots of land, resolving conflicts, arranging marriages, and officiating at ceremonies. Family members frequently consult them, and their advice is usually followed. Leadership is commonly passed down from father to son.

To increase national unity, the Nigerien government has urged people to strive toward creating a developing nation. In 1979 the authorities established a hierarchical structure of councils at the village, subregional (or arrondissement), regional (or departmental), and national levels. Except for village council members, the members of the other councils are either appointed or elected. Although the goal of the councils was to involve people in both economic and social development, many of the policies were not well received by the local people, leading to difficulties in implementing these policies.

Women of a clan pooling together their scarce pails of water.

FAMILY

A father and his two children. The boy on the left has a special haircut called the *zakara* (ZAR-kah-rah), which shows that the child is a male. The haircut resembles a rooster's comb.

Within the Hausa, intricate kinship relations develop through the male line, providing mutual support among the members in both rural and urban areas. The elders of a family intervene in every aspect of family life, such as promoting and arranging marriages for their juniors to strengthen family ties. Nonworking Hausa women stay in the family compound and only venture outside for medical treatment and family ceremonies.

Strong family ties among the Songhai group are illustrated by their large families: Married sons live with their parents. The living compound is divided into a main room for the father, a room for each of his wives, and rooms for his sons and families. While the men go to work, Songhai women do household chores, such as fetching water, preparing meals, cleaning the house, and looking after the children.

For the rural Tuareg, family life surrounds the tent or compound, which bears the name of the woman owning the tent. Tuareg women enjoy prestige in their society. When a girl marries, her elderly female relatives will give her a tent as her dowry. The tent becomes a powerful element in the couple's relationship, as the husband risks eviction from the tent when spousal disagreements occur. Tuareg society differs from other Muslim societies in its cultural practices and beliefs. Music, dancing, and private courtship conversations are part of their lives, as all of these are considered expressions of joy and life.

In urban areas there are more nuclear families, as young married couples prefer to live by themselves. A lack of housing is a major problem for the rapidly increasing population. Therefore living quarters often have to be shared with other family members, thus leading to overcrowding. With a rise in the number of homeless people, there are more thefts and social problems.

Despite these deterrents, many young people still leave their villages for work opportunities as well as the convenience of the cities.

MARRIAGE

Within each Nigerien community, marriage serves as a means of strengthening family ties and creating new ones. In Tuareg society, monogamy is the rule, but divorce is allowed. Tuareg parents do not arrange their children's marriages. Instead, playful courtship develops between young Tuareg boys and girls during community festivities.

Muslim, Hausa, and Songhai-Djerma men can have up to four wives. Divorce is allowed, although it is discouraged. In most villages parents arrange their daughter's marriage without her approval. Custom requires the man to pay a marriage gift to his future in-laws. Cases of arranged marriages between cousins often take place, and their failure causes rifts between family members.

Hausa polygamists are usually rich businessmen or respected elders.

The rural customs of Hausa groups require that the oldest son of a family be polygamous, bestowing honor, respect, and consideration to his parents. His first wife's parents will offer their other daughters—the wife's younger sisters—to be the man's second, third, or fourth wife. Today young, educated individuals oppose forced or polygamous marriages..

EDUCATION

Niger's system of education follows that of its former ruler, France. Although education in Niger is free, only a small fraction of children attend schools. In rural areas the distance to school is a major obstacle, since a junior high school is only available in the administrative center of an arrondissement, a high school in the administrative center of a department, and two universities, the Abdou Moumouni University in the capital city of Niamey and the Islamic University of Niger in Say. Before attending elementary school, children usually attend a school where they learn to recite the Koran in Arabic, the Muslim holy book, and the Islamic way of life.

A young woman who is available for marriage wears all her finest jewelry for the annual Gerewol celebrations.

Given their financial situation, many rural families do not send their children to school because they cannot afford to buy them stationery and books. In addition, some parents' groups view the establishment of schools with suspicion. As their children are taught a foreign language, parents are afraid that a social gap will be created between them, and that the school might "steal" their children from them. Thus they are not at always enthusiastic about sending their children to school. Some even go so far as to hide children from government officials. With recent education awareness campaigns targeted at the rural areas, parents are now reconsidering the option of sending their children to school. There has also been an important shift in the language used for primary instruction—from French to one of the four different languages that represent each major ethnic group. Many now realize the importance of education, as agricultural efforts have often been thwarted by changing weather conditions. Efforts are now being made to educate more rural children by establishing tent or hut schools. When the nomadic group moves, the school moves with them. Nomadic children are also being encouraged to attend schools through offers of hot meals. To help rural families further, the government has established elementary schools with room and board to house nomad children. One inconvenience of such boarding schools is the children's early separation from their parents. The children do not go home to visit during the school year.

Educated Nigerien women discussing their work.

Schooling is officially free and in principle compulsory for children between the ages of 7 and 12. At the end of secondary education students take the baccalaureate exam, which determines whether they can attend college. Today the total number of registered students in elementary schools is approximately 858,000, compared with 125,000 in high schools and 14,000 in tertiary education. Most of the teachers in elementary schools are Nigeriens, whereas professors in high schools and the universities are often French educators, teachers from other African countries, or U.S. Peace Corps volunteers. There are also private schools, which teach only in French. There also exist Koranic schools that specialize in the traditional teachings of Muslim theology, law, and Arabic history. Although the government grants scholarships to university students in Niamey, most of them come from well-to-do families and so do not need the money. Although antagonistic relations may exist among various ethnic groups, students from the different ethnic backgrounds generally treat one another with respect. Job prospects for graduating students are poor, forcing them to complete their training in European or other African countries.

LITERACY

One of the major obstacles to the education program is the extremely low literacy rate. Currently only 28.7 percent of Nigeriens are literate, one of the lowest literacy rates in West Africa. Approximately 42.9 percent of men can read, compared to 15.1 percent of women.

The government needs an education plan that embraces the country's varied language and cultural heritage and yet is still open to social and economic progress. If all five major languages were taught, Nigeriens would not be able to communicate with one another while doing business. To tackle this problem and increase literacy, the government established vocational schools to train teachers in the Hausa and Songhai-Djerma languages. The teachers are then hired to teach reading and writing in local languages to adults in the rural areas. However, the uneducated portion of society questions the viability of studying in local languages, as there are no job opportunities for people who are trained in them.

The limitations of the education system have forced some people to enroll in Koranic schools, which excel in teaching verse reciting. To expand Islam into sub-Saharan Africa, Saudi Arabia and Libya started to build several Islamic centers. In 1981 an Islamic University of Niger was built based in Say, 37 miles (60 km) from Niamey. A wide range of subjects, including philosophy, history, literature, banking, and finance, are taught with an Islamic perspective, and students also study in Arabic, French, and English.

In Koranic schools, students are taught the entire Koran, the Muslim holy book.

Children at a Koranic school in Zinder.

STUDENT MOVEMENTS

The student movement remains at the forefront of the political movement for social change in Niger. During the military rule of Kountché, students and trade unions led the popular strike that brought down the government. During the 1989 to 1990 school year, strikes and demonstrations for better equipment and improved facilities forced the national university to declare that year "a white year;" the academic year was canceled, and students had to repeat that year. In addition, the government's decision to send military troops to quell the student demonstrations resulted in many student deaths and injuries on the Kennedy Bridge in Niamey on February 9, 1990. In other cities students were beaten and arrested and then tortured. Because many of the victims were children of high government officials, protests spread quickly, and multiparty elections were demanded. As a result the constitution was suspended, the government dissolved, and a transitional government ruled until the first multiparty elections of 1993.

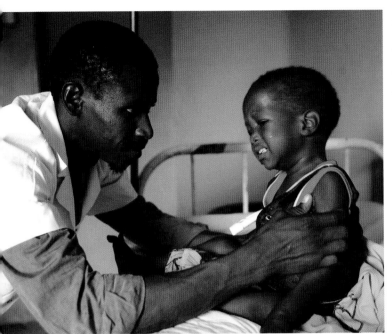

A nurse examines a child in the community health center in Niamey.

The student movement is also strong among Nigerien students who study in other African countries, such as Benin, Algeria, and Tunisia, where they frequently demonstrate, sometimes taking over the Nigerien embassies when their scholarships are not paid.

HEALTH

Health-care facilities in Niger are inadequate, and about a quarter of the population does not have access to health services. There are only a small number of health providers to serve the rapidly increasing population. In 2007 there was one physician for every 50,000 people. There is a shortage

of staff, and it is hard to obtain certain types of medicines. There are government hospitals in Niamey, Maradi, Tahoua, Zinder, and other large cities, with smaller clinics in most towns. In Niamey there are some private clinics, but only the well-off can afford to use them.

The main causes of death in Niger are illnesses caused by parasites, especially malaria. Niger falls within the African meningitis belt, with outbreaks taking place between the months of December and June.

The government's health program includes eradication of diseases in rural areas and health education. Children are given vaccinations against smallpox and measles. Diseases such as tuberculosis, malaria, trachoma, and leprosy remain endemic and continue to pose serious health problems. Major causes of the spread of these diseases include a lack of running water and sewage systems. To ease these health problems, some Nigeriens seek the help of local medicine men, who usually blame the illness on witchcraft and evil spirits. A total of 60,000 people in Niger are living with HIV/AIDS. So far there have been 4,000 deaths (according to a 2007 estimate). The highly pathogenic H5N1 avian influenza has been found in Niger, although it does not pose a severe risk. Life expectancy at birth for Nigeriens is 52.6 years.

Health volunteers educate Bella nomads, traditionally slaves of the Tuareg tribe, about how Guinea worm parasites are transmitted through contaminated water sources, and how to protect themselves from this parasite.

RELIGION

The Grand Mosque in Niamey.

CHAPTER 8

SLAM HAS PLAYED a vital role in uniting the ethnic mosaic of Niger, but problems are surfacing as rising fundamentalist movement attempts to use religious teachings to gain power. In Zinder, where they are a majority, Muslim fundamentalists have forced the government to forbid girls to wear Western-styled clothing, including short skirts. They also intimidate members of nongovernment organizations who provide health education to women.

More than 80 percent of the Nigerien population is made up of Sunni Muslims, and a small percentage is made up of Shia Muslims. The remaining are Christians or people who hold indigenous beliefs.

It does not matter where a Muslim is, as long as he or she can find a quiet place to pray. Here, a traveling Muslim stops his vehicle for his noon prayers. Devout Muslims have to pray five times a day.

Although the majority are Muslims, many Nigeriens remain attached to their animist customs and practice both beliefs. Some groups still hold on very strongly to their traditional practices. The Bororo Fulani and the Azna Hausa practice only their ancient cult religions. Although many Christian missions are found scattered throughout the country, only a small number of Nigeriens has converted to Christianity.

INTERPRETATION OF RELIGION

To Nigeriens religion provides a theoretical interpretation of the world. It can predict and control worldly events and supply answers to their problems. They believe that puzzling occurrences, such as sickness or financial success or demise, require explanations that religion can provide and reaffirm that order and regularity is the main objective of human interactions. Certain aspects of a person's life are also thought to be controlled by invisible natural forces or spirits, whose anger can be allayed or prevented by specific gifts and sacrifices.

In Niger faith in more than one religion is widespread among the population. Many Muslims practice pagan and animist customs and hold ancient ceremonies and rituals, which are against the teachings of Islam. Resorting to ancestral beliefs, witchcraft, and ritual spirit cults seem to be the result of the people's inability to find in the main religions answers to the worldly events that affect their lives. Many Nigeriens convert to Islam and Christianity because their leaders have converted, and they feel it is necessary to follow suit.

INTRODUCTION OF ISLAM

One of the earliest Muslim groups settled in Kanem, on the Chad frontier, after the fall of the Kharedjite rebellion in A.D. 947. By the 11th century other Muslim groups, as well as merchants, scholars, nomads, and craftsmen, had settled in the area. Trade relations soon developed between Kanem and the Muslim states of North Africa.

Although the Muslim religion suggested that slaves should be freed, trade caravans still brought them across Niger to Egypt and the Fezzan, a southwestern desert region in Libya and to Egypt. Within the country the

A mosque in Zinder.

social structure saw the creation of a slave class and a class of slave owners. The slave owners' ensuing economic prosperity increased the influx of merchants, Muslim scholars, and blacksmiths. Leaders of local clans turned into powerful rulers. They sought the help of Muslim scholars to expand their rule to adjacent regions, pitting one ethnic group against another. In one example in the 19th century, the Fulani waged a war against enemies of Islam and occupied Hausa states.

Several Sunni orders are predominant in Niger. The Tidjaniya, the largest group of Islamic scholars and teachers, has been the most popular among the Kanouri and the Songhai-Djerma since the 1920s. It was first established near Laghouat, Algeria, and during the French occupation, it spread south. Despite an initial opposition to French occupation of Niger, the order later reached a compromise with the French authorities from which it won favors. In contrast, the Sanussiya, a Sunni Sufi order, galvanized and spearheaded the Tuareg and Toubou groups' uprising against the French, who conducted harsh reprisals in return.

Nigeriens attending a Koran class.

A rural mosque in Niger.

Like other African nations, Niger sends Muslim pilgrims to Mecca, the Muslim holy site. Mecca is the birthplace of the Prophet Muhammad, whom Muslims believe was the last messenger of God. Muslims are taught that, besides the Koran, the Muslim holy book, Muhammad's sayings are the next most accurate revelations of Allah, their name for God.

Niger's constitution separates religion and state. However, it does not stop government officials from taking part in public religious ceremonies. Some Muslim men confine their wives to their house compounds, but the majority of women do not wear the veil or the *hijab* (hee-JAB), a piece of cloth covering their body, as do many Muslim women, such as those in the Middle East.

Unlike North African states, where aggressive fundamentalist movements have resulted in civil war, for example in Algeria, Niger has been able to achieve a compromise between its traditional customs and the Muslim religion. Nigeriens are happy to maintain this harmonious relationship.

CHRISTIANITY

In Niger less than 1 percent of the population is Christian. Christianity remains the religion of the towns, particularly Niamey. Many Christians are Europeans and non-Nigerien Africans who live in Niger. The main Christian denominations are Roman Catholic and Protestant. There are approximately 116,659 Protestants and 11,000 Roman Catholics in Niger.

Early missionary work in West Africa from the 15th to the 19th centuries focused on the communities on the Atlantic coast and countries south of Niger. The first Catholic mission in Niger was established in 1931 by Bishop Steinmetz of Upper Volta. In the 1940s African Missions of Lyon, known as the Fathers of Lyon, started their work in the city of Zinder. Unlike the precolonial Muslim missionaries and rulers in Niger who legitimized polygamy and traded slaves, Christian missionary workers insisted that Nigeriens become monogamous, eliminate superstition, and that slaves be freed. Christians focused their efforts on building religious schools and improving public health facilities and dispensaries to attract converts.

Bori musicians playing their spiritual tunes.

THE BORI CULT

Although the main religion is Islam, many Nigeriens still practice traditional cult rituals to seek relief from sicknesses or to explain unfortunate occurrences. These practices include the Yenendi (yay-NAN-dee), an ancient ritual to summon rain, sacrifices to appease or feed the gods, and sanctification of animals such as snakes, which followers believe look after the safety of their families and community as a whole.

The Bori (BOH-ree), meaning "spirit," is a spiritual cult of Niger that is practiced by a Hausa group called the Azna. The Azna are descendants of the Hausa who were chased out of the Aïr regions by the Tuareg and are one of the few groups who still retain their traditional rites.

The Bori ritual is a ceremony organized to call on the gods to intervene directly in worldly events and human affairs by possessing the body of an initiated woman or girl. Members of the cult include women from many roles in the rural society. They usually pray to the gods to drive away sickness and infertility.

The initiation rites are a monthly event. In the presence of the chiefs, *serkin* (SIR-kin) Bori, the women to be initiated are brought forward by the Bori queen, who is called *magajiya* (mah-GAH-jee-yah). The chiefs are the ones who officiate at the ceremony. The women start the ritual by dancing and continuing until they are in a frenzied trance. The ritual ends when the woman collapses on the ground, indicating that she is finally a Bori—and possessed by a spirit.

In areas such as Maradi and Niamey, the ritual was so widespread and the cult influence so strong that the political support of the Bori queens was much sought after in the early days of independence. The leadership of the Bori queens was instrumental in the creation of several women's organizations, such the Union of Nigerien Women.

A woman in trance dancing during a Bori ritual.

LANGUAGE

Nomadic Nigeriens having a conversation.

NIGER HAS BEEN INFLUENCED BY the cultures of Africa and France as well as the Muslim religion. Within this diverse heritage, language is the primary element that separates Nigeriens into several different groups.

Until France's occupation of the country, the main languages were Songhai, Hausa, and Tamasheqt, and smaller communities continued to speak a variety of dialects. During the French occupation a few schools that taught only French were built in the main cities, and the French-speaking people became an elite group.

Nigeriens generally speak two or three languages. Native languages such as Hausa allow for interactions within and outside ethnic groups. The French language allows Nigeriens to conduct business and communicate with the rest of the world. Nigeriens also use Arabic to recite verses of the Koran.

A sign in French, the official language of Niger.

Today there are three major languages in Niger—French as the official language, Hausa, and Djerma. The language of instruction in some schools and higher institutions is French, although recently primary schools have begun to teach in the main native languages of Hausa and Djerma. French remains the language used in the administration, industry, and finance. Most of the media, including television and radio broadcasts, and newspapers, use French. However, only a minority of the population speaks French.

There are at least 21 known languages and dialects in Niger, some of which are spoken by as few as 3,000 individuals. Each ethnic group speaks its own language, but Hausa has become the language for trade in most of Niger. A number of French-Arabic schools, some of them financed by the fundamentalist movement in the major urban areas, conduct two-thirds of their lessons in Arabic.

Children learning Arabic in Niger.

HAUSA

Hausa is the native language of about half the Nigerien population. The language belongs to the Chadic branch of the Afro-Asiatic language family. In the regions where it is spoken, Hausa has a uniform vocabulary and structure that make its variations mutually comprehensible.

At the time of the colonial conquest, people began to use the Roman script as a written form of the Hausa language. The first documents in Romanized form dated from the early 1930s and were introduced by the British administration. The second writing system is called *Ajami* (ah-JAH-mee), which means "non-Arab" or "foreigner" in Arabic. Ajami uses the Arabic system of writing with minor adaptations for particular Hausa sounds. At the beginning of the 19th century, Ajami allowed learned, religious people to write Islamic poetry in praise of the Prophet Muhammad and his followers and to extol Islamic doctrine. Much of Hausa writing today, however, uses Romanized characters for transcription, similar to the Hausa literature printed in Nigeria.

Hausa children having a conversation beside the morning fire.

SONGHAI-DJERMA

The language used by the Songhai-Djerma is the second-most spoken native language. It is also used in Mali, northern Burkina Faso, and Benin. The Djerma language belongs to the Songhai family of languages in Mali, and the Songhai language belongs to the Nilo-Saharan group of the Afro-Asiatic family of languages. Although Djerma is a dialect of Songhai, the Songhai people of Niger understand Djerma. The differences between the two are subtle, and people who are not well versed in them can hardly tell them apart. When combined, about 21 percent of the population speaks the Songhai-Djerma language.

The older Fulani can only speak Fulfuldé.

Songhai-Djerma and Hausa are considered the second languages of Niger. Other ethnic groups learn either Hausa or Songhai-Djerma, as required by their environment. These languages provide a tool of communication among the ethnic groups, including the Fulani, Tuareg, Kanouri, Toubou, Gourmanché, and other minorities, in markets and workplaces.

FULFULDÉ

The language of the Fulani or Peuhl is called Fulfuldé and is sometimes referred to as Fula or Pulaar. It is classified as a Northern Atlantic branch of the Niger-Congo family of languages. It is spoken by about 20 million people spread across almost all the countries of West Africa. Despite the extremely large region they inhabit, their dialects only differ slightly.

The Peuhl use two systems of transcription in their language: the Ajami, with slight modification for special Fulfuldé sounds, and Latin characters modified for special consonant sounds.

TAMASHEQT

The language of the Tuareg is Tamasheqt, which has its own alphabet called *Tifinagh* (tee-FEE-nahr). Tamasheqt is one of the *Amazigh* (ah-mah-ZEER) or Berber languages found in North Africa that belong to the Afro-Asiatic family. Because they are part of a matriarchal society, Tuareg women are responsible for passing on to their children their ancestors' language and its transcription. Women's duties include teaching the young the Tifinagh alphabet, which recently has become more popular with the advent of a strong movement to revive the Berber culture and language in Morocco and Algeria. Until recently Tamasheqt was limited to poetry and love messages. It is now used in more aspects of the Tuareg's lives. During their uprising, the Tuareg demanded political autonomy and greater control of their cultural and language heritage.

There are 420,000 speakers of Kanouri in Niger today.

A Tuareg couple speaking to each other in Tamasheqt.

OTHER LANGUAGES

There are other languages and dialects used by the smaller ethnic groups. The Kanouri and the Toubou languages belong to the Nilo-Saharan family, while Gourmanchéma, the language of the Gourmantché, belongs to the Niger-Congo family. The Kanouri people in Niger use the Ajami transcription to write Kanouri. The Toubou language is spoken by the Toubou people, who also speak Arabic.

A cameraman films a Télé Sahel broadcast.

LANGUAGE AND THE STATE

During its occupation of Niger, France did not try to impose the French language on Nigeriens. Only a limited number of schools were built. After independence, despite the government's efforts to improve literacy, only one-fifth of Niger's population spoke fluent French. Beyond the urban areas, French is rarely spoken today.

Since independence the Nigerien government has retained French as the official language, while actively promoting the native languages. The government has included news in the native languages in television broadcasts. The television station in Niger broadcasts daily news in Hausa and Djerma in between French programs, and it also broadcasts news in Tamasheqt, Fulfuldé, Kanouri and Toubou, Gourmanchéma, and Arabic. The few radio stations in Niger also provide slots for news in the native languages.

During a national conference in July 1991, a proposal to make Hausa the official language of Niger failed as the other major ethnic groups opposed it, especially the politically powerful Songhai-Djerma and Tuareg groups. As a result, the government has decided not to have one definite language or fixed education program but to recognize the languages of the five major ethnic groups.

THE MEDIA

Villagers enjoying a satellite television channel in Niger.

The media in Niger are made up of state-funded media as well as privately owned independent media. Because the population is largely illiterate and dispersed over great distances, radio is a popular way for the people to access news, information, and entertainment. Wealthier people in the cities have televisions, but the rural population cannot afford the expense of owning a television and often don't have access to electricity.

The Office of Radio and Television of Niger, or ORTN, is the state broadcaster of Niger. ORTN operates the Télé Sahel terrestrial television station, Radio Voix du Sahel radio network, and the TAL TV satellite station, which was formed in 2004. Ténéré TV is a private channel based in Niamey. Telestar, another channel operating from Niamey, is a pay-TV channel of Niger Television.

In addition to the national and regional radio services of the state broadcaster ORTN, there are several privately owned radio networks that total more than 100 stations. More popular radio stations include Anfani FM, Radio Sarounia, Radio et Musique, Radio Tambara. Nigeriens also have access to the BBC Hausa service and Radio France Internationale via satellite.

The government publishes a French-language daily newspaper, *Le Sahel*, and its weekend edition. There are approximately 12 private French-language weekly or monthly newspapers, some of which are affiliated loosely with political parties. Most prominent are the daily *La Nouvelle Tribune du Peuple;* the weeklies *Le Républicain*, *Le Canard Déchaîné*, and *Infos de l'Air;* and the *l'Evenement*, *L'Observateur*, and *Haské*, which are published every two weeks.

A Nigerien farmer listening to his transistor radio. Free-to-air radio stations are widespread and freely available to the masses.

PRESS FREEDOM AND REGULATION

In 1997 a press law was specifically introduced to control media criticism of the government. However, since the reinstallation of democracy in 1999, the media in Niger has been allowed more freedom and independence. Today Nigeriens are able to enjoy state, private, and international satellite radio and television. Some of the private-owned media, particularly the print media, can be highly critical of the government, in spite of strict state regulation, which includes harsh libel laws.

Although there is more press freedom, the government still controls the media when there is a state of emergency. During the coups of 1996, 1999, and in the 2000s, free and private media have been suspended, and many journalists were arrested and sometimes, imprisoned. More recently, as a result of the Tuareg uprising in 2007 to 2008, press freedom has been severely curtailed.

In 2007 the independent Radio Agadez was closed by the government, and foreign journalists were banned from entering the northern part of the country. Two local journalists were imprisoned, charged with helping the Tuareg rebels. The journalist Moussa Kaka was held for more than a year for granting a radio interview to Tuareg rebel leaders, before being

Grémah Boucar, director of the independent radio station Radio Anfani or Anfani FM and publisher of the bimonthly news magazine Anfani, *received the International Freedom Award of the Committee to Protect Journalists on November 24, 1998, in New York. Boucar and Radio Anfani were the target of attacks by military troops during General Maïnassara's rule. Boucar's radio station was shut down in 1996 and ransacked by military troops in 1997 because of his criticism of the government's actions and his opposition to press censorship. Boucar and some Radio Anfani journalists have been taken into custody several times. Boucar is an example of Africa's emerging independent broadcasters and journalists who oppose Africa's authoritarian and intolerant governments despite threats from the authorities.*

Radio Anfani was launched in 1994 during the administration of Niger's first democratically elected president, Mahamane Ousmane. The radio station quickly attracted a large Nigerien audience. While a number of journalists covered local news, Radio Anfani also rebroadcast news programs from the Voice of America, the British Broadcasting Service, and Radio Deutsche Welle.

provisionally released. Some stations have even been shut down simply for reporting on the conflict in the north.

In 2008 and 2009 the government continued its crackdown on the media. In August 2009, Abdoulaye Tiémogo, an editor of a private weekly newspaper, *Le Canard Déchaîné*, was sentenced to prison over the newspaper's allegations of government corruption and its criticism of the decision to issue an international arrest warrant for exiled former Prime Minister Hama Amadou on corruption charges. In April 2009 managing director Abibou Garba and editor in chief Seyni Amadou of the privately owned Dounia Media Group in Niamey were also arrested and detained for allegedly disseminating false information.

International groups such as Amnesty International and the International Federation of Journalists and Reporters Without Borders have lodged complaints that these restrictions are in violation of Niger's commitments to international law and press freedom.

ARTS

Tuareg camel bags beautifully made from decorative leather.

ART PLAYS AN IMPORTANT ROLE in Niger's economy. Artisans in each ethnic group excel in making one or two types of artifacts, depending on their living environment and way of life. Pottery making, particularly earthenware water jars, is the forte of Djerma women.

The Songhai make blankets and weave mats. Tuareg artisans make excellent silver jewelry with elaborate motifs and leatherwork with exquisite designs, as well as sculpt wood and make utensils, tent equipment, and saddles. Fulani women are adept at engraving calabashes, weaving, and basketry. The Hausa produce some fine woven textiles, as well as exquisite, tightly woven baskets.

Painted terracotta pots for sale at a market in Niger

Niger enjoys a vibrant traditional and contemporary arts scene and is well represented in the fields of dance, literature, storytelling, painting, theater, cinema, and music. Many artists use their work as a platform to provoke thought and discussion about Niger's social and political issues.

Nigerien men playing their traditional drums.

Although Nigerien arts have retained their traditional forms, modern Nigerien painters have drawn inspiration from Western and Muslim styles and integrated them in their paintings. Exhibitions of Nigerien art are usually held in the Niger Museum, which is located in Niamey. Built in 1958 the museum exhibits many artifacts and works of art by the different ethnic groups.

MUSIC AND THE TUAREG

Playing music and singing are important elements in any Nigerien social event. Music is used to celebrate human events, such as births, weddings, circumcisions, and religious holidays. The musicians and their audiences share in a creative performance, to experience a communal activity, and to express feelings of camaraderie.

As guardians of traditions and customs in the Tuareg society, women have greatly contributed to the Tuareg cultural heritage. As a result, music is not a man's sole privilege; women play music as well, although their styles differ. Women play most traditional instruments, except flutes.

The women's musical styles include the *tindé* (TUHN-day) and the *ezelé* (ay-ZAY-lay). The *tindé* is the most common musical rhythm in Niger. It is created by a drumlike instrument called a *tindé* that is made with a mortar with goatskin stretched across its opening. In the *tindé* performance, the player also sings to the rhythm she makes with the instrument. *Ezelé* is a dance music for women played to accompany male dancers.

LEATHERWORK AND JEWELRY

Tuareg artisans, called *inadan* (EEN-ah-dan), are excellent craftspeople, making silver jewelry, saddles, camel bags, tools, utensils, talismans, and water containers from goatskins. They also specialize in leather products, such as traditional money purses and shoes. Leather shoes are made from the rawhide for protection from scorpions, thorns, and sand fleas. The soles must be wide to allow support on the fine sand. Decorative patterns are intricate, and when dyed leather is used, these items become art pieces that can be worn only at special occasions. From the Saharan scrub and trees, artisans make ladles, bowls, and beds. Ladles are embroidered with dyed wool, apart from leather.

Tuareg artisans create a wide range of rings, anklets, and amulets. But the best-known jewelry item is the Agadez silver cross, called a *teneghelt* (te-NER-gelt), sometimes referred to as the Cross of the South (of Europe). Several designs exist, with each pattern representing a clan or confederation. In Niger nearly every city is represented by its silver cross.

Tuareg craftsmen working on a camel saddle.

HAUSA FOLKLORE

Because of the nation's low literacy rate, Niger's folklore is best preserved in the form of oral tales, legends, and proverbs. Riddles, poetry, and the lyrics of old songs also contain some age-old stories. The literature of the Hausa people is vast and varied. As the Hausa converted to Islam, they also began to transcribe poetry in Ajami script. The main characters in a Hausa folk tale can be an animal, a man, a woman, a hero, or a villain. All folk tales attempt to highlight some traditional values and morals of their culture. Other tales include legends, which can be historical accounts of former rulers or stories of spirits. The Hausa believe in the presence of powerful spirits that intervene in their daily lives.

WALL DECORATION

The Hausa are a very creative people, and their art is visible in their houses. To add sparkle to the dull earthy tones of their homes, the Hausa paint colorful motifs on the exterior walls. The patterns used are greatly influenced by

Decorative facade on a building in Niamey.

Known as Jeliba the Great Griot, Jibo Baje still narrates the epics of Africa accompanied by the warm music of his lute. To learn more about his country's traditions and to better preserve its heritage, Jeliba has expanded his sources and studied the different versions of the epics. In his search he has traveled beyond Niger to consult elders. Having already benefited from his traditional teaching, Jeliba now uses his sharp voice and his music to sing the common heritage and culture of Niger, reminding his audience of bygone days.

Islamic and African styles. Original African motifs underline much of the decoration found in Hausa textile embroidery and wall decorations. Elaborate and intricate decorative patterns are also part of Hausa architecture. Early geometric mud decorations mainly adorn doors and other openings, and they were probably the result of old charms used to ward off evil intruders. Later the decoration expanded to include entire walls.

GRIOTS

Africa's oral traditions can be compared with the abundant libraries in Western countries. To retain this oral tradition, every ethnic group has griots, who are masters of the spoken word. During cultural celebrations in villages and cities, the eloquent griots will share with their audience many centuries-old folktales, stories, proverbs, poetry, legends, riddles, and historical epics. Their moving tales have captivated Western researchers interested in the cultural history of Niger and West Africa. These scholars have recently started to concentrate on learning more about the rich Nigerien customs and traditions, as well as their literature, history, sociology, and anthropology.

A griot comments on the reenactment of the Hausa War.

 As a poet, storyteller, and musician, the griot is a walking encyclopedia for his people. He knows all the historical and cultural facts about his people,

ALPHADI: AN AFRICAN FASHION DESIGNER IN PARIS

Born to a Tuareg father from Timbuktu in Mali and a Tuareg mother from Niger, Seidnaly Sidhamed Alphadi is considered the representative of new African fashion. He skillfully combines the exotic and traditional colors and styles of Africa to attract Western taste. He is one of the few fashion designers from Africa whose style has penetrated the international fashion scene in Paris and New York.

Even though he was born with talent, Alphadi worked very hard to become what he is today. While preparing for a doctorate in tourism from a school in Paris, he took evening classes in fashion and design and worked as a model for Giorgio Armani. On his return to Niger he held the position of director of tourism promotion but resigned soon after. He headed for Paris and New York to complete his training in fashion design. In 1986 he introduced his first collection and has since won countless fashion prizes and medals. In 1987 the Federation Française de la Couture et du Prêt-à-Porter bestowed upon him the award of Best African Designer. Other awards include the Chevalier de l'Ordre de Mérite de la France in 2001 and the Kora Fashion Award-South Africa in 1999.

In 1999 Alphadi expanded his label to include a new sportswear line called Alphadi Bis. *He also worked with well-known jeans brand Wrangler to create* Alphadi Jeans *to appeal to a younger crowd. In 2000 he made history by launching* l'Air d'Alphadi, *the very first perfume by an African fashion designer.*

Alphadi is certainly the world's best-known African fashion designer. He has been successful in his ambition for his work to be seen by the world and understood in Africa.

OUMAROU GANDA

Oumarou Ganda was a Nigerien director and actor who introduced African cinema to an international audience in the 1960s and 1970s. Ganda was born in Niamey in 1935 and belonged to the Djerma ethnic group. He met French anthropologist and filmmaker Jean Rouch when he was living on the Ivory Coast (Côte d'Ivoire), and Rouch introduced him to film and the cinema. Ganda played the lead role in Rouch's film Moi un Noir *in 1958.*

When Ganda returned to Niamey, he became involved in the Franco-Nigerien Cultural Center. After receiving training in directing, camera, and sound, he became an assistant technician. Ganda's first autobiographical film, Cabascabo, *based on his experiences in Indochina, was written in response to a screenplay competition organized by the center in 1968.*

His most famous film, Le Wazzou Polygame *(1970), won the first FESPACO (The Panafrican Film and Television Festival of Ouagadougou, or Festival panafricain du cinéma et de la télévision de Ouagadougou) Festival Best Film Award. This film deals with polygamy and forced marriage and is critical of the powerful in Nigerien political society. His other films include* Saïtane *(1972) and* L'Exilé *(1980). Ganda also made documentaries. He died of a heart attack on January 1, 1981.*

After his death, as a way to honor Ganda and his work, a major cultural center, Le Centre Culturel Oumarou Ganda, was named after him. Another posthumous honor included the FESPACO African Feature Film Award, named the Oumarou Ganda Prize.

community, and country. He is the transmitter of a wealth of knowledge from one generation to another. Sometimes he is an official member of the royal court of a local chief, living permanently among his community. In some villages he lives apart from the local community but is allowed to speak freely. A griot can also be employed to work in a village or a city. He is hired for family celebrations and electoral campaigns. There are griots in all the Songhai-Djerma, Hausa, and Kanouri ethnic groups.

The griot is both feared and respected in Nigerien society. According to African wisdom, words are God's gift to a griot. They are considered sacred, and Nigeriens believe they contain magical powers that the griot can summon in ritual chants and rhythmic incantations to feed nature's spirits and forces. A griot may also extol the glories of powerful rulers or scoff at past incidents. Some griots have special relationships with their masters, acting as advisors. In the past, during wars, the griots would accompany their masters, usually rulers of a region, to battlefields so that they could tell stories to boost the boldness and strength of the soldiers.

LITERATURE

Currently Nigerien authors publish very few books in local languages. Until recent decades the country's culture was conveyed orally from one generation to another. During family gatherings, the older folks would impart to the young their knowledge of the history and traditions of Niger and their ethnic group, as well their own experiences.

Books on display in a bookshop.

As the African saying goes, "An old man who dies is a library that burns." Many Nigeriens are starting to realize the historical disconnection that can result from the lack of writing. This accounts for the increase in Nigerien literature in French that can be found today. The authors record the rich oral traditions and customs, giving the words of older generations an everlasting life span.

The first Nigerien ever to publish a book before independence was Ibrahim Issa. He wrote *Les Grandes Eaux Noires* (*The Large Black Waters*). His most popular work is a book of poetry called *La Vie et Ses Faceties* (*Life and Its Jokes*) that contains the exploits of great African leaders, such as Samory, Issa Korombey, Béhanzin, and Lumumba. The book is written in the style of an African traveling poet and musician.

There is no Nigerien literature that is written in English.

Another prominent writer is Boubou Hama, the former president of the National Assembly, who died in 1982. Born in 1906 he was the author of more than 40 books, including important works on ancient empires, as well as traditional folktales and essays. In 1970 he was awarded the Grand Prix Littéraire de l'Afrique Noire, the great literary prize of sub-Saharan Africa, for his own autobiography, *Kotia Nima*.

More contemporary writers include Oum Ramatou and Hélène Kaziende. Oum Ramatou is a writer born in Niamey in 1970. She wrote *Le Regard* and *Désiré*. Hélène Kaziendé was born in 1967 in Niger. She now lives in Togo. She is a teacher and a journalist. She published a novel, *Aydia*, in 2006. Her short story "*Le Déserteur*" ("The Deserter"), published in 1992, was awarded a prize at the literary competition organized by the radio station Africa No 1.

Etran Finatawa of Niger performs during the WOMAD world music festival.

MODERN MUSIC AND ART

Even though Nigeriens are very interested in traditional art, they do not condemn modern art forms. On the contrary, contemporary art is embraced by younger Nigeriens. In Niamey, groups of young singers—for instance, the group Black-Dapss—perform Nigerien rap music, using music to convey messages about social problems, such as drugs and AIDS. The freelance theater company Les Tréteaux du Niger, formed in 1994, has been innovative. Instead of waiting for the public to attend plays, the freelance comedians decided to seek their audience wherever they may be. Their repertoire includes six original creations adapted from Molière, Corneille, and Shakespeare, and they have performed in towns and villages in Niger, Africa, and Europe. Rissa Ixa is a Tuareg painter born in Ayorou. His paintings are records of the vanishing Tuareg life. His goal is to preserve cultural heritage by educating society.

LEISURE

Nigerien men resting on a mat.

NIGERIENS ARE A VERY sociable people. They enjoy taking part in festive gatherings, such as weddings and birth ceremonies. Communal gathering places, including markets, are not only a place for daily grocery shopping but are also busy and lively arenas where, among other things, friends and associates meet and spread latest news and fashion trends.

Most Nigeriens spend their leisure time around events that bring together friends, family, or the community. Such social events contribute to a sense of ethnic identity.

Tuareg men and children playing a game in the sand.

Locals enjoy watching the intensity of a traditional wrestling match in Agadez.

Besides traditional activities, modern sports, such as soccer, have caught on in Niger. Many people now enjoy watching matches either live or on television. City dwellers enjoy going to the movies.

SPORTS

Traditional wrestling is a popular sport. Many people flock to the championship games held by the Ministry of Sports and Culture. The coveted prize is a ceremonial saber that is awarded to the winning team. Long-distance running has also gained some fans since three Nigeriens—Gabirou Dan Mallan, Issoufou Ouseini, and the 1996 winner, Moussa Yeli—took top positions in the 11th 13-mile (21-km) run in Abidjan, Côte d'Ivoire, in 1998. A promising sportsman from Niger who has received international recognition is Abdou Alassane Dji Bo. He is a judo professional who won the third position in the half-lightweight competition of the African Judo Championships in 2004 and 2006. In the 2005 African Judo Championships, he received the silver medal in the same category. Other well-known sports people in Niger include skillful soccer players such as Ismael Alassane and Kassaly Daouda, who play for Niger's national football team. Popularly called the "Mena," the national soccer team in Niger represents the nation in international matches.

The Nigerien government has taken an active role in the promotion of sports in the country. So far, it has supported sports organizations and organized games, promoted traditional sports, and formed teams to take part in international games. In 1972 Nigerien lightweight boxer Issaka Daboré won the bronze medal at the Olympic Games in Munich. He also won several medals in various African competitions. The 2008 Summer Olympics in Beijing, China, were Niger's 10th Olympics game. Niger sent five athletes to compete in five events—tae kwon do, men's 50-meter (164-foot) freestyle, women's 50-meter (164-foot) freestyle, and the 400-meter (1,312-foot) and 1,500-meter (4,921-foot) track competitions.

Among modern sports, soccer is the preferred sport of Nigeriens, offering a source of entertainment for men and young boys. It has become the most popular sport in Niger because of the bonding that results from the various African and World Cup competitions that attract millions of spectators. With a soccer league that organizes tournaments for teams from different regions, Niger is able to participate with other African countries on a regular basis. In December 2005 Niger hosted the fifth Francophone Games, which included sports such as track and field events, basketball, boxing, soccer, judo, table tennis, and traditional wrestling.

Boys playing soccer in Niamey.

Nigerien men playing a card game.

ENTERTAINMENT

Household electronic equipment has brought dramatic changes to Nigerien leisure. Many wealthier urban dwellers now own television sets, DVD players, and stereos. American television series, broadcast on Nigerien television, are very popular among English-speaking Nigeriens. Urban teenagers also enjoy watching Hindi dramas and action movies.

Every large city has an outdoor cinema where Nigeriens can enjoy the latest movies. In Niamey movie festivals, conferences, and art shows are held at the Oumarou Ganda Cultural Center or the French Cultural Center.

DARA

Both young and old men play *dara* (da-RAH), a game similar to checkers. There are usually two players. Pits of the dum-dum tree fruit are used as pieces. To play, rows and columns of holes are made in the sand. One player puts the pits in his share of holes, while his adversary uses small millet twigs in his holes. The objective is for each player to move his pieces to the farthest row of holes.

SHARRO

Sharro (SHAR-raw) is a sportlike activity practiced by rural Fulani youngsters when they enter manhood. It is an endurance and bravery test and is performed by two opponents. According to his partner's age and category, the giver violently hits his partner with a tree twig or a stick a certain number of times. His partner, the receiver, must endure the pain, pretending not to be hurt. He must also smile at the audience to prove his excellent control over pain. A year later the roles are reversed. The competition can continue for many years.

Because Sharro is a dangerous game, and people have been badly injured, the Nigerien government has forbidden it. Although it is not practiced at public festivals and ceremonies in the towns anymore, some people still practice it secretly outside the villages.

Fulani nomads engaged in a friendly fight.

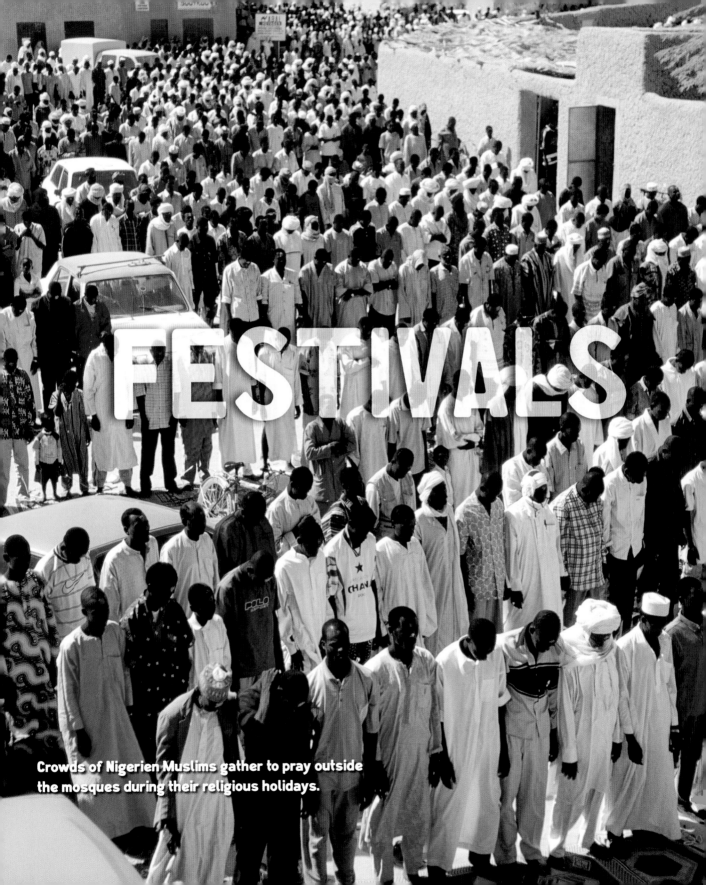

FESTIVALS

Crowds of Nigerien Muslims gather to pray outside the mosques during their religious holidays.

NIGERIENS LOVE AN EXCUSE to meet friends and family to eat and enjoy themselves, so the numerous festivals in Niger provide them with many opportunities to gather for a feast. Whether the holidays are religious or secular, there is always plenty to eat.

MUSLIM HOLIDAYS

Muslim religious holidays include Eid al-Fitr and Eid al-Adha. Celebrations follow the lunar calendar, so they are held on different dates every year. With the Muslim year being 11 days shorter than the year of the Gregorian calendar (the civil calendar that is used by most of the world), it takes about 33 years for the holy month of Ramadan to fall in the same month again. During Ramadan, Muslims fast from sunrise to sunset, abstaining from eating, drinking, and smoking.

A Hausa minstrel celebrates the Tabaski (tah-BAH-skee), a Muslim festival.

Nigeriens are proud of their varied and colorful festivals, which take place throughout the year, attracting local residents as well as tourists. Festivals can be religious, traditional, or simply based on the enjoyment of the arts. Nigeriens from all backgrounds enjoy participating in their unique festivals.

117

Eid al-Fitr, or the Feast of Eating, marks the end of Ramadan, and is celebrated with family and friends. On this day the men wake up early in the morning to gather in the mosque for prayers. After prayers, relatives and friends visit one another, and children are given money and treats. A large feast is served for lunch.

Eid al-Adha, or the Feast of the Sacrifice, is known in Niger as Tabaski. It commemorates the Prophet Abraham's willingness to sacrifice his son and is the highlight for those who have completed the hajj. The hajj is a pilgrimage to the holy city of Mecca in Saudi Arabia.

For male Muslims, Eid al-Adha starts with a morning prayer, led by an imam, or Muslim spiritual leader, at the mosque. At the end of the prayers, the imam will slaughter a ram, a signal to the followers that they can go ahead and slaughter their own rams. The sacrifice of a ram symbolizes giving oneself to Allah. The meat is usually distributed to friends, neighbors, and poor people. During this time Muslims are reminded to be compassionate and help the poor and needy.

THE BIANOU FESTIVAL

To celebrate the Muslim New Year, the Bianou festival is held in the city of Agadez to commemorate the birth of the Prophet Muhammad and the mysterious construction of the Great Mosque of Agadez. It is celebrated for three days and starts with *ettebel* (ET-bel), a drumming and a call from the minaret. As crowds gather, the *ettebel* players appear, followed by Tuareg dancers who perform spinning dances in their long, blue robes.

Agadez has been a sultanate since 1449, and the festival is held in the sultan's palace. Tuareg people from neighboring cities come to take part in the grand camel race, which includes more than 200 traditionally dressed Tuaregs riding camels. To start the camel race, women musicians play *tindé*. The race begins outside the city, and the finish line is the courtyard at the sultan's palace. In the evening crowds gather to listen to a *takamba* (TAH-kahm-ba) performance, music played by a traditional guitar player. Women start to gather in a circle, and the men start dancing. The women then join them in the dance.

SALT CURE FESTIVAL

Every fall the Bororo Fulani and the Tuareg nomads gather after completing a yearlong seasonal migration and hold the Salt Cure Festival in In-Gall and Teguidda-n-Tessoum, where green pastures are abundant. In-Gall is located in an oasis with palm groves and date plantations. The name "salt cure" comes from the salt that is contained in the new grass, which is an essential part of the animals' diet. The nomads believe that the salt cure fattens the animals.

During the festival the Tuareg, dressed in traditional clothes, hold camel races, and artisans exhibit their exquisite leather and wooden artifacts and jewelry. To offer support, the government regularly takes part in the celebration by distributing sugar, millet, and tea to the nomads. To kick off the celebrations, Tuareg women play *tindé*, a traditional Tuareg musical instrument, and sing. While they perform, the men proudly ride their camels around the racing grounds.

The Bororo group of the Peuhl or Fulani also holds their annual beauty contest in conjunction with the Salt Cure Festival. Known as the Gerewol, the cult of beauty reaches its apex during this celebration, in which only men are allowed to participate. After spending many hours donning traditional makeup and decorating themselves with their most beautiful clothes and jewelry, the Bororo men line up to perform a dance.

Tuareg perform a dance called "le Dramague" accompanied by spikes and swords during the annual Salt Cure (*Cure Salee*) Festival in Niger. The nomad tribes in Niger (Tuareg and Fulani) gather for one week on the Niger side of Sahara because of the rich salt deposits and to rest, fatten their animals, give them the "salt cure," and enjoy music, dance, and camel racing.

Bororo men, with their painted faces and decorative dress, get ready to dance during Gerewol.

The participants, who have decorated their faces with pale yellow powder and painted the edges of their eyes with black kohl, dance forward, graciously shifting and lifting their weight from one foot to the other while clapping their hands and singing. As they dance, they will smile at a group of young unmarried women who are the judges. It is customary for the dancers to keep their eyes wide open to emphasize their facial beauty. After the dance the judges mix with the young men and choose the most beautiful. However, if the men are displeased with the judges' decision, fights can break out. The Nigerien government has attempted to stop this celebration because it often ends in violence.

WRESTLING CHAMPIONSHIP

With the help of the Ministry of Sports and Culture, the championship games for traditional wrestling have become the most popular sport among Nigeriens. Every year the championships attract hundreds of athletes and more than 20,000 spectators from the region. Daily media coverage, including many hours of live television broadcasting, demonstrates the popularity and the importance accorded to traditional wrestling in Niger.

Traditional Nigerien wrestling is the forte of the sedentary Hausa and attracts many fans every time the games are held. Established in 1975 the championship games draw large crowds to the wrestling grounds. Television and radio viewership also reaches a peak during the games.

STORYTELLING FESTIVAL

In November 2009 Niger hosted the sixth edition of the international storytelling and oral arts festival dubbed "Gatan-Gatan" at the Dogodoutchi culture center, 186 miles (300 km) south of Niamey. The idea was developed by members of the collective of artists Jawabi to celebrate the culture of Niger. Artists and professional storytellers came together from 11 African and European countries to attend this five-day cultural event. The objective of the event was to promote Nigerien culture, particularly to preserve the value of storytelling as a comprehensive art which encompasses music, songs, poetry, and dancing. Artists from Belgium, Benin, Cameroon, Côte d'Ivoire, Central African Republic, France, Mali, Niger, Nigeria, Senegal, and Togo attended seminars on the traditional oral art. Artists and participants of the festival were also able to go on an excursion to Lougou, an animist sanctuary located 31 miles (50 km) from Dogondoutchi—the birth place of Saraounia Mangou, who was both an animist queen and war figure of Nigerien history. Cooking and traditional plaiting competitions were organized as well as performances of traditional and modern music.

Bororo women decorate the beds given by their husbands after the birth of their first child at the annual Worso Festival.

Nigerien wrestling is somewhat different from the common forms of wrestling. It is more a mix of Japanese sumo wrestling and Greco-Roman wrestling. At an early age children in the rural areas start practicing, but the strongest wrestlers come from urban areas. The winner may not always be the heaviest or strongest. Besides physical training, preparation for the wrestling championship includes psychological exercises, animist rituals, and prayers. The sport is also practiced in several other West African countries.

The preliminary selection of contestants is held in the morning in the administrative centers of the territorial departments. Each department holds its own games and selects a 10-member team that will represent it at the national level. The national championship takes a week to complete. During the championship games, besides the matches, wrestlers parade in the arena, showing their muscles, while musicians entertain the spectators, and the camel riders perform their camel dance.

To win the championship, the wrestler must win seven rounds. One round is won when his opponent falls on the sand. The winner is awarded a sword, a horse with a harness, a traditional outfit, and a check that he receives from the hands of the Nigerien minister of Youth and Sports. International competition now takes place during the Jeux de la Francophonie and the Championship of African Lutte Traditionnelle, which was established in 1996.

OTHER FESTIVALS

There are other traditional and colorful festivals in Niger that take place throughout the year. Yenendi is a rain-calling traditional ceremony where worshipers request that the Earth be showered with rain before the fields

Most Nigeriens do not work on New Year's Day, which falls on January 1. However, because most of them are Muslims and celebrate only the Muslim New Year, the Christian New Year is just a public holiday for them, not an important occasion. Easter Monday, Labor Day (May 1), and the Proclamation of the Republic (December 1) are national holidays. Other important celebrations are on April 15, which commemorates the coup that ousted Diori; August 3, the anniversary of independence; and December 18, Republic Day, which is the republic's birthday.

are planted. It is usually performed when there is a drought. The ceremony is called for by the village spokesman, who invites the villagers to gather around a sacred place outside the village, usually under a big gao tree. All the villagers join in the procession, dancing and singing while waiting for the rain to come.

Hotungo is the annual celebration of the nomads, held in October. Wassankara is a political comedy festival held in April. Hawan Kaho literally means "riding the horns." Traditionally Nigerien butchers would try to get hold of the horns of an angry bull and ride it. This festival is organized in November and attracts thousands of spectators as well as tourists.

Men dancing during a festival in Niger.

FOOD

Various types of dried produce, vegetables, and canned goods on sale at a stall in the center of Tahoua in Niger.

T HE TRADITIONAL CUISINE OF NIGER is varied. By using only staples such as millet and sorghum, Nigerien women are able to create several delicious dishes for every meal. The flavors and tastes of each dish can be very different for the various ethnic groups.

STAPLES

Millet is Niger's main staple. The traditional midday meal is *fura* (FOO-rah), a millet porridge prepared with water or milk, spices, and cooked

Tuareg women at a village in Niger pound millet during the day, which they will then make into porridge for dinner.

flour. The pastoral Fulani rely on dairy products, such as yogurt, milk, and butter, but they also eat millet, sorghum, and corn porridge. Besides millet the Hausa diet also consists of sorghum and corn. The Tuareg nomads eat mainly grains. Dairy products, such as milk and cheese, and fruits, such as dates and melons, provide additional nutrition.

MEAT AND VEGETABLES

Nigeriens prepare meat dishes mainly for special occasions and holidays. In markets grilled mutton brochettes are popular snacks that provide energy. Fresh or dried vegetables, such as okra, onions, peppers, spinach, tomatoes, squash, pumpkins, eggplant, sorrel, and baobab leaves, are added to sauces or porridge. Fish is a favorite among the people who live near the Niger River and Lake Chad. Nigeriens enjoy snacks prepared with meat and grilled tripe, and cakes made with fried beans or peanuts. Mangoes, dates, and melons are usually consumed in large quantities when they are in season.

An outdoor restaurant in Niamey.

The different ethnic groups have different food and table customs. The Fulani consume meat but do not slaughter their healthy cows. The Songhai men and women eat separately. To increase children's food consumption, the custom is to eat from the same gourds. During cricket season, women snack on fried crickets, referred to as "desert shrimps."

TYPICAL MEALS

A vendor sells millet and corn flour at a district market in Niamey.

Nigeriens' typical meals consist largely of porridge, pancakes, or pastes made from millet flour. Pancakes are eaten at breakfast, porridge at noon, and pastes topped with other ingredients and sauces are consumed in the evening.

A normal midday meal in a rural or poor urban family consists of boiled millet or sorghum and buttermilk. Sometimes spices or sugar are added. In the evening, *tô* (TOH), a popular West African dish made with white millet or sorghum balls, is eaten with different kinds of sauces. The sauces are made from green leaves, onions, tomatoes, dried legumes, spices, and meat, if there is any. If there is chicken, dried beans and sorghum usually complement the dish. In the rice-planting region along the Niger River, rice is eaten with local spices and spinachlike herbs and groundnuts. Dishes with smoked or dried fish are cooked with local ingredients. Most rural families have two meals a day. For the poorer ones, one meal per day is common.

In urban areas wealthy families lead a more Westernized lifestyle. They also have the opportunity to try Western food. For them a meal may consist of plenty of rice prepared with a tasty vegetable sauce and eaten with meat or fish. In contrast to the rural people, urban families can afford to have three meals a day.

The eating habits of the nomads in Niger are similar to those of the farmers. The main difference is that, compared with their fellow countrymen, they consume more milk and dairy products, such as butter. The dairy products are produced from cow's milk, which is also used to trade for grains. The nomads also eat a substantial amount of meat, because from time to time, they slaughter some animals from their herds.

NIGERIEN FOOD TRADITIONS

Families supplement their regular meals by eating raw roots, tubers, manioc, and sweet potatoes. Fruits and vegetables are expensive, and meat, eggs, and fish are only prepared during family celebrations and holidays.

Depending on the ethnic groups and their socioeconomic conditions, religions forbid the consumption of some foods, such as pork and alcohol. The meat also has to be fresh, and the animal must be slaughtered in accordance with Islamic principles. Tradition also forbids pregnant women and children to eat certain foods, such as eggs.

Preparing tea. Everyone is expected to drink three cups of tea. The host will be extremely offended if his or her offer is refused.

SIPPING TEA

In many Muslim countries in Africa, a traditional custom is to drink hot and foamy tea. To the Tuareg, tea drinking is a solemn affair. It is a ceremonial display where each step of the preparation is carried out with care. In addition to its stimulant properties, tea offers drinkers an opportunity to hold long conversations, especially near a campfire while enjoying the starry desert night. To make tea, two pots are used. The steaming tea is poured from one pot to the other so that foam appears. The foam protects the drinker's lips.

DRINKS

Among the Tuareg, *aragaiga* (ah-RAH-gay-gah) tea, which is Chinese green tea, is the preferred drink after a meal. Mint is usually added to the tea, and three cups are always drunk. The Tuareg say that the first cup of tea is strong, the second cup is soft, which means it is slightly weaker than the first, and the third cup is light and is usually offered to the children. During special ceremonies and on journeys, the Tuareg drink *egherdjira* (ER-er-jee-rah), a drink prepared with pounded millet, dates, milk, and goat cheese. It is very rich and is drunk with a ladle.

In the cities, people sip strong, hot coffee for breakfast. Sometimes the coffee is mixed with milk. Soft drinks, found at every food outlet, are popular. They include Coca-Cola, Sprite, Fanta, and local soft drinks. In the villages, a local alcoholic drink, *bourkoutou* (BOOR-koo-too), made by fermenting millet, is very strong and is favored by the Hausa. In the large cities, such as Niamey, French-owned stores carry food products, such as yogurt and ice cream, specially imported from Europe. Because these products are very expensive, few Nigeriens can afford to enjoy them.

Girls carrying trays of nuts and olives on their heads at a market.

PEANUT STEW

4 servings

2 pounds (900 g) boneless lamb
   stew meat

3 onions, sliced

3 ½ cups (875 ml) of water

1 ½ (7.5 ml) teaspoon salt

3 large tomatoes, quartered

3 chili peppers

1 cup (250 ml) of peanut butter

2 cups (500 ml) of beef bouillon

3 to 4 cups (750 ml to 1 L) of cooked rice

3 hard-boiled eggs

- Put the lamb, the onions, and 3 cups (750 ml) of water in a saucepan. Bring to a boil and then simmer, covered, until almost tender, for about an hour.

- In a separate pan, combine tomatoes, chili peppers, and ½ cup (125 ml) water.

- Bring to boil and simmer 10 minutes.

- Add the peanut butter and the beef bouillon to the tomato mixture.

- Add the tomato mixture to the meat.

- Simmer until tender.

- To serve, put a helping of rice in each soup bowl. Put an egg in center of rice and cover with stew.

DATE SAUCE

4 servings

1 pound (450 g) lean steak, cut into bite-sized pieces

¼ cup (60 ml) oil

6 fresh tomatoes, chopped

2 medium onions, chopped

2 medium green peppers, chopped

2 garlic cloves, minced

1 cup (250 ml) dried, pitted dates, chopped

2 tablespoon (30 ml) tomato paste

2½ cups (625 ml) tomato sauce

1 teaspoon (5 ml) salt

1 teaspoon (5 ml) pepper

½ teaspoon (2.5 ml) ground cumin

A pinch of ground cinnamon

- Brown the meat in a little oil and remove from the pan.
- Add the tomatoes, onions, and green peppers to the pan, adding the remaining oil.
- Simmer until the vegetables form a mush then add the garlic, spices, meat, dates, tomato paste, and tomato sauce.
- Simmer for around 40 minutes until the sauce is thick and the meat is tender. If desired add a little water to prevent the dish from drying.
- Serve on a bed of rice or couscous.

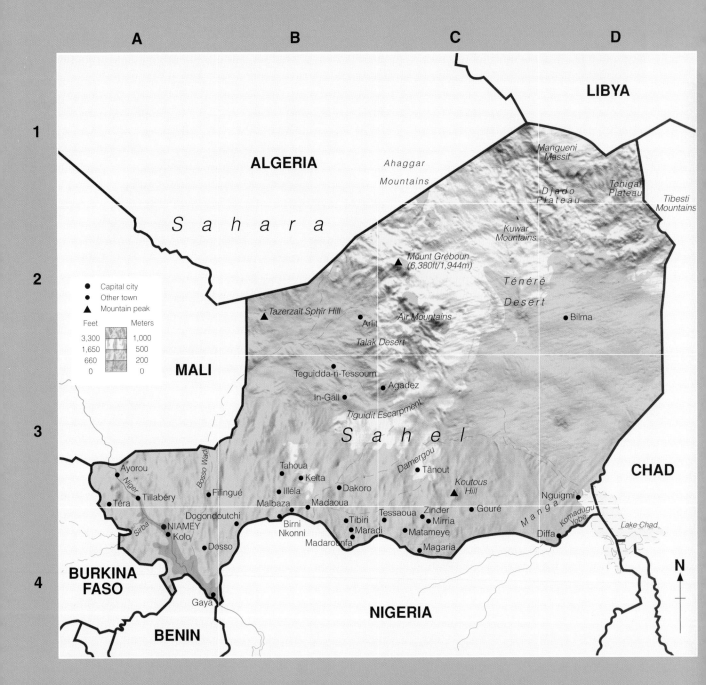

	A	B	C	D

1

ALGERIA

LIBYA

Ahaggar

Mangueni Massif

Mountains

Djado Plateau

Tchigaï Plateau

Tibesti Mountains

S a h a r a

Kuwar Mountains

2

▲ Mount Gréboun
(6,380ft/1,944m)

Ténéré Desert

● Bilma

▲ Tazerzaït Sphîr Hill

● Arlit

Air Mountains

● Capital city
● Other town
▲ Mountain peak

Talak Desert

Feet	Meters
3,300	1,000
1,650	500
660	200
0	0

MALI

Teguidda-n-Tessoum ●

● Agadez

In-Gall ●

Tiguidit Escarpment

3

S a h e l

Bosso Wadi

Damergou

CHAD

Ayorou ●

Tahoua ●
● Keïta

● Tânout

Niger

Tillabéry ●

Filingué ●

● Illéla

● Dakoro

Koutous Hill ▲

Nguigmi ●

● Téra

Malbaza ●

Madaoua ●

Tessaoua ●

Zinder ●

● Gouré

Manga

Komadugu Yobe

Dogondoutchi ●

Birni Nkonni ●

● Tibiri

● Mirria

Diffa ●

Lake Chad

Sirba

● NIAMEY
Kolo ●

● Maradi

Matameye ●

Madarounfa ●

Magaria ●

● Dosso

BURKINA FASO

4

Gaya ●

NIGERIA

N
↑

BENIN

MAP OF NIGER

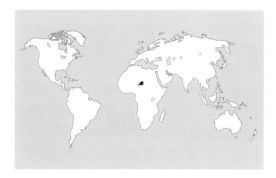

ECONOMIC NIGER

Agriculture
- Cotton
- Millet & sorghum
- Peanuts
- Rice
- Sugarcane
- Tomatoes
- Wheat

Natural Resources
- Coal
- Gold
- Limestone
- Oil
- Salt
- Tin
- Uranium

Manufacturing
- Cement plant
- Slaughterhouse
- Textile plant

Services
- Airports
- Tourism

ABOUT THE ECONOMY

OVERVIEW

Niger shares a common currency, the CFA franc, and a common central bank, the BCEAO, with seven other members of the West African Monetary Union. A landlocked sub-Saharan country, Niger remains one of the poorest countries in the world, according to the United Nations Development Fund. Its fragile economy relies mainly on subsistence crops and livestock. Recurring drought cycles and desertification exposes its agricultural economy to erratic harvests. Lack of rainfall and a rapidly growing population have put enormous pressures on the economy. Fortunately Niger has some of the world's largest uranium deposits and is rich in other natural resources and minerals. Niger relies on international debt relief provided by organizations such as the International Monetary Fund, which allows essential spending on basic health care, education, rural infrastructure, and other programs aimed at poverty reduction. Economic growth may be achieved in the future by the exploitation of oil, gold and coal.

GROSS DOMESTIC PRODUCT (GDP)

$10.75 billion (2009 estimate)

CURRENCY

Communaute Financière Africaine franc (XOF)
US$1= 441.89 XOF (2009 estimate)

GDP GROWTH

3.2 percent (2009 estimate)

AGRICULTURAL PRODUCTS

Cowpeas, cotton, peanuts, millet, sorghum, cassava (tapioca), rice, cattle, sheep, goats, camels, donkeys, horses, poultry

INDUSTRIES

Uranium mining, cement, brick, soap, textiles, food processing, chemicals, slaughterhouses

MAJOR EXPORTS

Uranium ore, livestock, cowpeas, onions

MAJOR IMPORTS

Foodstuffs, machinery, vehicles and parts, petroleum, grains

MAIN EXPORT PARTNERS

Japan 80.4 percent, Nigeria 8.5 percent, France 2.9 percent (2008 estimate)

MAIN IMPORT PARTNERS

France 19.4 percent, Nigeria 8.6 percent, China 8.5 percent, French Polynesia 7.6 percent, Belgium 5 percent, Cote d'Ivoire 4.9 percent (2008 estimate)

WORKFORCE

4.7 million (2007 estimate)

INFLATION

0.1 percent (2007 estimate)

EXTERNAL DEBT

$2.1 billion (2003 estimate)

CULTURAL NIGER

Bura
The archaeological site of Bura is situated in the Tillabéri region. The site consists of burial mounds, altars, and numerous individual necropolises with coffins adorned with terracotta statuettes. In 2006 Bura was added to the UNESCO World Heritage Tentative List.

Niamey
The sprawling capital city of Niamey is full of attractions, including the Small and Great markets. Other attractions include the Great Mosque, the National Museum (including botanical gardens and a zoo), and the Hippodrome, where horse and camel races often take place.

Agadez
Known for its famous camel market, Agadez is a busy market town. Historical buildings in the city include the 16th-century Grand Mosque, built in 1515, and the sultan's palace. Agadez is also well known for its craftsmanship, including its silver and leatherwork.

Aïr and Ténéré Natural Reserves
Covering more than 297,298 square miles (770,000 square km) this vast area of Niger is a protected sanctuary. The reserve is home to a unique collection of flora and fauna as well as stunning landscapes and wildlife. Declared a World Heritage Site in 1991, it includes the volcanic rock mass of the Aïr. In 1992 it was added to the World Heritage in Danger List.

Tillabéri
Situated on the Niger River, Tillabéri is an important market town and administrative center. It is famous for its wildlife, particularly its herds of giraffes.

Ayorou
A riverside town on the Mali frontier, Ayorou is well known for its Sunday market at the old trading station. It is known for its animal market and wildlife, including hippopotami and birds.

"W" National Park
Declared a World Heritage Site in 1996, the Nigerien part of "W" National Park, situated just outside of the capital of Niamey, is flourishing with abundant birdlife and wildlife, including buffalo, elephants, lions, hyenas, jackals, and baboons.

Dosso
The town of Dosso, founded in the 13th century, has an exceptional palace and a lively village square. Its palace–Djermakoy's palace and museum–was nominated as a UNESCO World Heritage Site in 2006.

Maradi
Although Maradi is mainly an industrial city today, its rich past is evident in its ancient buildings, including the Dan Kasswa Mosque and the Katsinawa Provincial Chief's palace. Other interesting attractions include the Centre Artisanal in the Sonitan Quarter that showcases traditional crafts, and the Maradi Grand-Marché, which is a large market, open daily, selling all kinds of agricultural goods. In Maradi there are also ruins from the Sokoto Empire.

Zinder
Zinder was the capital of Niger until 1927. Highlights of the city include the Birnin Quarter and the Zengou Quarter, filled with a maze of alleyways. Some of the best examples of typical Hausa architecture can be found here. Near the center are the sultan's palace and the Grande Mosque, where it is possible to enjoy a great view of the city from the minaret.

OFFICIAL NAME
Republic of Niger

NATIONAL FLAG
Three equal horizontal bands of orange (top), white, and green with a small orange disk (representing the sun) centered in the white band; similar to the flag of India, which has a blue-spoked wheel centered in the white band

LAND AREA
489,062 square miles (1,266,670 square km)

CAPITAL
Niamey

ADMINISTRATIVE DIVISIONS
Agadez, Diffa, Dosso, Maradi, Niamey, Tahoua, Tillabéry, Zinder

HIGHEST POINT
Mount Bagzane (6,634 feet/2,022 m)

POPULATION
15,306,252 people (July 2009 estimate)

POPULATION GROWTH RATE
3.68 percent (2009 estimate)

LIFE EXPECTANCY
Total population: 52.6 years
Male: 51.39 years
Female: 53.85 years (2009 estimate)

BIRTHRATE
51.6 births per 1,000 population (2009 estimate)

DEATHRATE
14.83 deaths per 1,000 population (2009 estimate)

ETHNIC GROUPS
Hausa (55.4 percent), Songhai-Djerma (21 percent), Tuareg (9.3 percent), Peuhl (8.5 percent), Kanouri Manga (4.7 percent), and others 1.2 percent (2001 census)

RELIGIONS
Muslims: (80 percent); other (indigenous beliefs and Christians): 20 percent

MAIN LANGUAGES
French (official), Hausa, Djerma

LITERACY RATE
28.7 percent

INFANT MORTALITY RATE
116.66 deaths/1,000 live births

NATIONAL HOLIDAY
Independence Day (August 3)
Republic Day (December 18)

TIME LINE

IN NIGER	IN THE WORLD
1890 France occupies Niger.	**1939** World War II begins.
1958 Niger becomes autonomous republic of the French Community.	
1960 Niger becomes independent; Diori Haman is elected by parliament to serve as president.	
1968–73 Severe drought devastates Niger's economy, including its livestock and crop production.	
1974 Diori Herman is overthrown in military coup led by Lieutenant Colonel Kountche.	
1987 Ali Seybou, the armed forces chief of staff, succeeds Kountche, who dies of a brain tumor.	**1986** Nuclear power disaster at Chernobyl in Ukraine
1989 A new constitution brings Niger back to civilian rule, but under a one-party system; Seybou is elected president. Ban on parties is lifted.	
1990 Seybou legalizes opposition parties in response to a wave of protests and demonstrations. Tuareg people in the north organize rebellion.	
1991 After a constitutional conference removes Seybou of his powers, a transitional government under Andre Salifou is established.	**1991** Breakup of the Soviet Union
1992 New constitution allowing multiparty elections is ratified.	
1993 Mahamane Ousmane is elected president and his coalition wins a majority of seats in parliament.	
1995 Ceasefire between the government and the Tuareg's Revolutionary Armed Forces of the Sahara.	
1996 Ousmane ousted in a coup led by Colonel Ibrahim Mainassara, who wins presidential election.	

IN NIGER	IN THE WORLD
1997	**1997**
The Democratic Renewal Front, a hardline Tuareg group, signs peace accord with government.	Hong Kong is returned to China.
1999	
Following the assassination of Maïnassara, Major Daouda Wanke assumes power. Mamadou Tandja is elected president.	**2001**
2002	Terrorists crash planes in New York, Washington, D.C., and Pennsylvania.
Soldiers mutiny unsuccessfully in the east and in the capital of Niamey.	**2003**
2004	War in Iraq begins.
First-ever local elections take place. Parties supporting the president win majority of the seats. President Mamadou Tandja wins a second term.	
2005	
Widespread protests over tax increases. International Court of Justice awards Niger most of the river islands along its disputed border with Benin.	
2007	
Government declares alert in the north, giving the army greater powers to fight Tuareg rebels.	
2008	**2008**
The 110-million-year-old fossils of two previously unknown species of flesh-eating dinosaurs are discovered in Niger's desert area. Police arrest former prime minister Hama Amadou on charges of embezzling state funds.	The first black president of the United States, Barack Obama, is elected.
2009	
Government and Tuareg rebels of the Movement of Niger People for Justice (MNJ) agree to end hostilities. President Mamadou Tandja suspends constitution and assumes emergency powers after Constitutional Court rules against his plans for a referendum on whether to allow him to seek a third term.	
2010	
Rebel soldiers attack and depose Tandja in a coup d'état, establishing a military junta called the Supreme Council for the Restoration of Democracy (CSRD)	

GLOSSARY

Ajami
Modified Arabic script formerly used by the Hausa. It means "non-Arab" or "foreigner."

Amazigh
Refers to the Berbers. The word means "noble man."

azalay (ah-ZAH-lay)
Long annual camel salt caravans that traverse the Ténéré Desert.

Bori
Spirit possession cult practiced by Hausa and African diaspora of North Africa.

dara (da-RAH)
A checkers-like game played with pits of the dum-dum tree fruit and short millet twigs.

Gerewol
A weeklong festival with dances and a male beauty contest held by the Bororo Fulani.

griot
Local bard, poet, narrator, and musician.

hajj
The pilgrimage to Mecca.

hijab
A piece of cloth worn by a Muslim woman. It covers the entire body except the eyes.

imam
A Muslim religious figure who preaches at a mosque.

magajiya (mah-GAH-jee-yah)
Bori queen, who leads the women to be initiated in the Bori ritual.

sharro (SHAR-raw)
A physical competition that tests the endurance and bravery of Fulani teenagers.

tagelmust (tag-ERL-moost)
A piece of long, indigo cotton cloth worn by the Tuareg men to veil themselves.

teneghelt (te-NER-gelt)
A term used by the Tuaregs. It refers to the silver cross of Agadez.

Tifinagh
An ancient script of the Berber language still used by the Tuareg.

tindé (TUHN-day)
Musical rhythm created by a tambourine-like instrument made with a mortar and goat skin stretched across the opening and attached with strings to two pieces of wood.

Yenendi
A traditional ritual to summon rain when the rains fail to come at the end of the dry season.

FOR FURTHER INFORMATION

BOOKS

Geels, J. *Niger* (Bradt Travel Guides). Chalfont St. Peter, UK: Brand Publications, 2006.

Jenkins, M. *To Timbuktu: A Journey Down the Niger.* London, UK: Robert Hale Ltd., 2002.

Kashi, E. *Curse of the Black Gold: 50 Years of Oil in the Niger Delta.* Brooklyn, NY: Powerhouse Books, 2008.

FILMS

Dan Balluff Film and Video Production. *Niger,* 2005.

MUSIC

Etran Finatawa. *Tekana (Niger)* from album *Think Global: Celebrate Africa!* Think Global/World Music Network, 2009.

Group Bombino. *Guitars from Agadez (Music of Niger)*, vol. 2, Sublime Frequencies/Forced Exp., 2009.

Various Artists. *Niger—Charles Duvelle Collection/1961*. Kora, 2000.

Various Artists. *Niger: Chasseurs du Dallol Mawri (Hunters of the Dallol)*. Ocora, 2005.

WEBSITES

BBC News, http://news.bbc.co.uk/1/hi/world/africa/country_profiles/1054396.stm

CIA: The World Factbook—Niger, www.cia.gov/library/publications/the-world-factbook/geos/ng.html

Eden Foundation, www.eden-foundation.org/project/desertif.html

Encyclopaedia Britannica, www.britannica.com/EBchecked/topic/414746/Niger

IPOAA—Indigenous People of Africa and America Magazine, http://ipoaa.com/short_facts.htm

Nation Master, www.nationmaster.com/country/ng-niger

Niger Watch, http://nigerwatch.blogspot.com/

BIBLIOGRAPHY

BOOKS

Ayaji, J. F. A. and Michael Crowder. *History of West Africa*, vol. 1, 3rd ed. New York: Longman Group, 1985.

Delgado, Samuel. *Historical Dictionary of Niger*. Metuchen, NJ: Scarecrow Press, Inc., 1996.

Hale, Thomas A. *Griots and Griottes: Masters of Words and Music*. Bloomington, IN: Indiana University Press, 1999.

Keenan, Jeremy. *The Tuareg*. New York: St. Martin's Press, 1977.

Malio, Nouhou, Maiga, Mounkaila, and Thomas A. Hale, eds. *The Epic of Askia Mohammed* (African Epic Series). Bloomington, IN: Indiana University Press, 1996.

Manning, Patrick. *Francophone Sub-Saharan Africa: 1180—1995*. Cambridge, England: Cambridge University Press, 1998.

Van Offelen, Marion and Carol Beckwith. *Nomads of Niger*. New York: Abradale Press, 1993.

Riesman, Paul. *Freedom in Fulani Social Life*. Chicago: University of Chicago Press, 1977.

Stoller, Paul. *In Sorcery's Shadow: Memoir of Apprenticeship among the Songhay of Niger*. Chicago: Chicago University Press, 1989.

WEBSITES

Fashion Window, www.fashionwindows.com/news/alphadi/default.asp

International Federation of Red Cross and Red Crescent Societies, www.ifrc.org/where/country/cn6.asp?countryid=127

Irin News, www.irinnews.org/Africa-Country.aspx?Country=NE

Join Africa.com, www.joinafrica.com/countries1/Niger/people.htm

Maps, www.mapsoftheworld.com

Nations of Encyclopedia, www.nationsencyclopedia.com/Africa/Niger.html

Net for All, www.netforall.com/servlets/ShowSite?reqtype=domain&admin=NIGER&folder=Environmental_Issues

Niger Delta Solidarity, http://nigerdeltasolidarity.wordpress.com/

Parliamentary Center of Canada, www.parlcent.ca/africa/gender/niger

PBS, www.pbs.org/wnet/africa/explore/sahel/sahel_overview.html

Population, Flags, and Capital Cities for All Countries, www.population-of.com

Social Studies for Kids, www.socialstudiesforkids.com/articles/geography/nigerriver.htm

UNESCO, www.UNESCO.org

UNHCR, www.unhcr.org/pages/49e484ee6.html

U.S. Department of State, www.state.gov/r/pa/ei/bgn/5474.htm

WHYCOS, www.whycos.org/rubrique.php3?id_rubrique=27

Wildlife Extra, www.wildlifeextra.com/go/news/termit-niger.html#cr

INDEX